MW00803049

Beyond Xs and Os: My Thirty Years in the NFL

Jim Hanifan
with
Rob Rains

Sports Publishing L.L.C.
www.sportspublishingllc.com

Director of production: Susan M. Moyer
Project manager: Jim Henehan
Dust jacket design: Kerri Baker
Developmental editor: Kipp Wilfong
Copy editor: Cindy McNew and Susan M. Moyer

All photos courtesy of Jim Hanifan.

ISBN: 1-58261-670-1

Printed in the United States of America

Sports Publishing L.L.C.
www.sportspublishingllc.com

This book is dedicated to my wife of 45 years, Mariana. She encouraged and supported me through the years, through all the peaks and valleys.

The same is true of my two children, Kathleen and Jim. I thank them for their love, faith and adaptability.

Thanks also to my brother Steve for his friendship and constant support.

Contents

Foreword

By Dan Dierdorf

The first time I met Jim Hanifan was when Don Coryell was hired as the head coach of the Cardinals in 1973 and Jim came with him from San Diego State. The team rented out a restaurant and invited all the players who lived in town to come meet the new coaches. So, amazingly, my first meeting with Jim Hanifan ended up in a bar. Who would have imagined that?

We developed an instant bond. It was like we were separated at birth, only his birth was many years before mine. I loved his enthusiasm, I loved his ability to talk about so many things other than football. I quickly discovered that Jim Hanifan is a remarkably intelligent, well-read, learned man. He can talk to you about the classics, he can talk about a trap play, he can talk about life, a Broadway play or the latest top five books on *The New York Times* bestseller list. He is a remarkably diverse man, but he is first and foremost a football guy. Sooner or later it all comes back to football.

Jim Hanifan would have been a tremendous professor at any university in America. He would have been a corporate leader heading up a management team and succeeding in business. Everyone who has even been in contact with Jim on the football field is just fortunate that he applied his energy and expertise to the sport of football. We were all blessed because of that.

I played in the NFL for 13 years, and Jim was either my offensive line coach or head coach for 10 of those years. People who really played for Jim would die for him. I'm sure there are a lot of people who attempted to play for Jim, and if they didn't try hard, were shown the door. Jim demanded that you love the game. He only wanted people who loved the game. If you loved the game you could be quirky, you could be crazy (if your name was Conrad); Jim didn't care. If you loved the game and had a passion for the game, you were his kind of player. If you weren't a very good player but still had a passion for it, you had a friend for life in Jim Hanifan.

All you have to do is go to any gathering of football players and stand back and watch the group when Hanifan enters the room. It's like bees to honey, sooner or later they all make their way to Jim. They want to hug him, they want to be hugged, they want a slap on the back, they want to reminisce.

We used to look forward to getting up and going to work every day. It sounds corny, but we really did, just to be around him.

He was a tremendous technician. He was a firm believer that your technique is your only friend. When things started going bad on the field, when you were not doing well and the guy across from you was giving you a tough time, chances were it was because you were doing something wrong. He used to drill us over and over and over. His favorite word was repetition. I soaked it up, I loved it. I loved being that type of player. Jim convinced me that if I took a pass set and before I took it, I stepped in a tray of paint, if I took 100 pass sets, there would only be one set of tracks. He really made me believe it.

Jim kept it fun. It is hard work. Football is a unique game. It's the only sport where practice really sucks. Games are easier than practice. Normally, in other sports, practice is not that high pressure. But in football you're beating the crap out of each other, especially linemen. Jim kept it interesting, whether he was telling a story, with how approachable he was, or his infectious enthusiasm. Jim is an unbelievable competitor. We really believed in our heart of hearts that if he could, Jim would have run onto the field. We used to tell him, how about if we set it up for you and the defensive line coach of the other team to meet at the 50-yard line and duke it out in pregame warmups? I would have bet on Hanifan every time.

Would I have been a Hall of Famer without him as my coach? Probably not. Maybe the best answer is, "Who did I ask to present me at the Hall of Fame?" They tell you to think about who had the most profound impact on your professional career. It's the ultimate thank you. I thought about some different people, but when I thought who was the person who had the biggest influence on my professional career, it wasn't even close. There was no one who could rival what Jim Hanifan did for me.

I don't think any career assistant coach will be selected for the Hall of Fame, but he's in mine. Every time I see a player who played for Jim, they are so jealous because I live in the same town and get to see him. Russ Grimm is the line coach of the Steelers, and he played for Jim in Washington. When I see him, everybody in the stands looks at us on the field, standing there, laughing and slapping each other on the shoulder. They think we are old friends, but truthfully I don't know Russ Grimm. But he's one of Hani's boys, and so am I. That makes us great friends.

My best memories of Jim are that my girls think of him as their uncle. We try to see him and his wife, Mariana, each summer at their cabin at Lake Tahoe. To sit in the living room in his cabin and see the looks on my kids' faces as he talks and tells stories about everything except football is really fascinating.

People have come up to me on different occasions and asked if I would like to be a coach. I am quick to tell people you really demean the coaching profession when you ask me a question like that. I am flattered, but you have to understand, coaching is a profession. These are men who have honed themselves and learned things over decades and are now applying them like any other profession. No one can just say, "I'm going to be a coach," and go coach. It doesn't work like that. We've seen examples of that, and those people were lost. It takes experience, desire and a love of teaching. Jim has all of those skills.

One time Jim was holding one of his weekly news conferences and someone asked him a question about his strategy. "What do you know about football?" he asked in return. "Do you have any idea how much time we spend in meetings, working on the tendencies of the other team?" Then he went around the whole room and asked every writer and every TV guy about their football experience. He got to one of the TV guys who had to admit to the room that he never played football. Then Jim asked his cameraman, "What about you?" The cameraman said he had played high school football, and Jim said, "You can ask me a question, he can't."

Jim wears his emotions on his sleeve. He is quick to laugh and quick to cry. When he left St. Louis to go back to San Diego after the 1978 season, it meant he was leaving me behind. He had to go. I knew it was best for him, but it was painful. We went out the night before his flight to San Diego and ended up sitting on the hood of a car at 3:30 in the morning in tears because neither of us could say goodbye. It turned out he was only gone a year, and I got hurt in the second game and missed the rest of the season. The day I heard that Bill Bidwill hired him as the head coach of the Cardinals was one of the greatest days of my life.

We had a party at my house, and Jim got there about 9 p.m. There must have been 100 people or more there, and that baby didn't stop until dawn. Then Jim went right to work, nothing new about that.

I hope our last gathering ends up just like the first, with the two of us bellied up to a bar somewhere, laughing and enjoying life. That's what Jim deserves, and I want to be lucky enough to be there with him.

St. Louis, Missouri
June, 2003

Acknowledgments

I would like to acknowledge all of the coaches I have worked with over the years. I started to compile a list, but as you can imagine, it proved to be rather lengthy.

So thanks to all of my fellow coaches at Yuba City Junior College, Charter Oak High School, Glendale Junior College, the University of Utah, the University of California, San Diego State, the St. Louis Cardinals, the San Diego Chargers, the Atlanta Falcons, the Washington Redskins and the St. Louis Rams.

Introduction

Trying to find a book that interests a sixth grade boy can be difficult. I never will forget the day I was in the library when I was that age and happened to come across *Bernie Bierman's Guide to Football*.

I checked it out, went home and read it. And re-read it, back and forth, cover to cover. I think I memorized every word in that book.

Determining what your life's work is going to be can be a very imposing task, especially for a young boy growing up just after World War II. I knew, though, even without really thinking about it, that I was hooked on football.

From the time I was 14 years old and a freshman in high school, football has been a big part of my life. When that ball is kicked off to start a game, I still have the same feeling today that I had standing on that field on a Friday night as a freshman at Covina High School in southern California more than 50 years ago. There is no feeling in the world like it.

Seeing that field all lit up as you ran out from the locker room, you just went "wow." There was a special smell in the air, and what you were really taking in was the essence of the game. The adrenaline was pumping, and, really, the same statement is as true for me today as it was then.

When that ball is kicked off, this is a battle, the nitty-gritty, let's go! I have been on that field as a player, and I have stood on that field as a high school coach on Friday night, as a college coach on a Saturday afternoon and as a professional coach on

Sundays and Monday nights. I can't think of anyplace I would rather be. It's almost magic.

I just flat-out know there is nothing that can replace that feeling. My coaches told me, and I have told my players, that part of the beauty of football is that you never know when that big play is going to come, but you had better be ready, because it might be your turn to be the star, to make that play that determines whether your team wins or loses the game.

It can come on offense, or defense, or on special teams, you just never know. Your team can be the favorite, or you can be the underdog, but that ball is a spheroid, and because of that, that darn thing can go goofy and do some crazy things. I have seen it happen.

This game is played by humans, and no human is perfect. People make mistakes, and that sometimes determines the outcome of games. You can be running with the ball, and somebody comes right at you, closes his eyes, and happens to hit the ball at the right angle and it pops loose. All the drills in the world can't prepare you or prevent that.

That is the kind of thing you hope happens if you are a big-time underdog. I've seen it happen in high school and I've seen it happen in Super Bowls. That's why you hear the media say the best team doesn't always win. It's a cliché, but it's true, and it's the reason the game is so special.

It is also special because of the people, the players, the coaches, the owners, the management and the fans. I have been fortunate to work with some great people over all of my years in the game, and I am honored and privileged to call them my friends. Coaches like Don Coryell, Joe Gibbs, Dick Vermeil, and Mike Martz. Players like Dan Dierdorf, Conrad Dobler, Tom Banks, Joe Jacoby, Russ Grimm, Ed White, Jackie Smith, Keith Wortman, Ernie McMillan, Jimmy Lachey, Raleigh McKenzie, Mike Kenn, Tim Kearney, O.J. Anderson, Roy Green, Willard Harrell and all of my current linemen on the Rams, as well as countless others.

Owners like Gene Klein and Jack Kent Cooke were great to me. Bill Bidwill gave me the opportunity to be a head coach in the NFL and I will always be grateful to him for that.

My long list of friends that I have made because of the game also include the legendary Pappy Waldorf, my college coach at California; Pappy Cofield, my Army coach in Europe; Dr. Robert Hines, the doctor on our Army team in Europe; Buzz Bemoll, my high school football coach; Doc Sooter, my high school basketball coach; Ray Willsey, my teammate and later the head coach at Cal; Bing Bordier, a former USC player and my teammate in the Army; Bill Koman, a former player at North Carolina and with the Cardinals. All of these men have been big influences on my life.

My wife Mariana and our kids, Kathy and Jim, have made countless sacrifices because of the demands the game puts on a coach, and I thank them for that. They have helped me live a dream, doing the one thing in the world I can imagine myself doing, coaching football.

My daughter Kathy, after graduating from college and entering the work force, probably gave me the very best compliment a father can receive. She told a group of fellows, "I'm going to do something like what my father does." When they questioned her about what she meant, she said, "He loves what he does, and that's what I'm going to do. It isn't a job to him. It's not work. It's exciting and meaningful to him."

From the moment I read that book in the sixth grade, whether I consciously said it or not, I knew my life was going to be spent in football. I'm glad I made that choice.

CHAPTER 1

Getting an Education

It doesn't matter if it is a high school, junior college, major college or professional game, football is still football. Those high school kids out on the field under the lights on Friday night are trying to do the same thing the college kids are trying to do on Saturdays and the pros on Sunday and Monday night. Football isn't a hard game. We—the coaches, the fans, the players, the media—can make it complicated, but the game has been played fundamentally the same way for decades and will continue to be played the same way far into the future.

When I was a kid growing up in southern California, we didn't look up to pro athletes the way kids do today. Kids today have too much access to information. They can watch all of the games on television or get the stats off the computer. All we knew to do was play, and try like hell to win the game.

I was thrilled when my coaches and teammates elected me captain of our team at Covina High School, and I was determined to take the role seriously. One day we scrimmaged against another team before the season started. That team was made up of guys who, back in grammar school, were bigger and more mature than we were. They kicked our tails in everything. On this day, however, things were different. We were the same size or bigger than they were. I went berserk all afternoon and just created havoc. I was going "Ha, wait a minute, the shoe's on the other foot now. Run my way. Come on over here." I was yelling at them, and our coach asked me afterward, "Jim, why did you do that? What got you so riled up?" I said, "Coach, when we were in the seventh and eighth grades, those guys beat us to a pulp. It was payback time." He understood.

My high school career did not start off that well. My freshman year, practice started a couple of weeks before school. I didn't go out for the team, because I was too shy. I did show up for practice the first day of school, but it was almost my last day, too.

I got home about 6:30 p.m. and my dad was waiting. We lived on a chicken ranch, with maybe 3,000 or 4,000 chickens, and there was always a lot of work to do. My old man was upset. He said, "Where have you been?"

I told him I had been at football practice, and he said, "That will be the last practice you go to. I want you here by 2:30 so you can get your chores done." I did what all kids do in that situation, I went to talk to my mom.

"Dad wants me to come home after school and says I can't go to football practice," I said. She looked at me and said with her deep Irish brogue, "Jimmy, let me ask you this. Do you think you're going to be good at that?" I said, "Yes, I think I will be very good." She said, "Well, if you're going to be good at it, you should do it."

When my brother and I left the table after dinner that night, my mom and dad had a big argument. They didn't usually argue, and when they did, my dad usually got the last word. He didn't win this one. She said if the boys think something is important and that they have a chance of success with it, then they should get that opportunity.

My parents had both come over to this country from Ireland. My father, Jim, was a much bigger man than I am. He was about 6-foot-5 and trim. He had been an all-Ireland Gaelic football player, and actually won a medal for winning the world championship in 1902 at Wembley Stadium in London. I still have that medal, and wear it at times. I'm very proud of it.

Dad was going to be a priest. He went to the seminary and made it all the way to the final vows in Rome before changing his mind. Obviously I'm glad he did, or I wouldn't be here. He went to England and took a job as a clerk in a legal firm and worked there for a few years, saving his money.

His two brothers had already left Ireland for the United States, and they kept writing him letters telling him what a great country it was and how everyone had opportunities. They wanted him to join them. He finally did, and the first night he was in this country, staying at a boarding house in New York, somebody stole his wallet and all his money. He then went to Boston, got a job as a longshoreman, and worked long enough to save money for the train trip out to Nevada, where his brothers were working.

The three of them ended up buying a ranch in Fallon, Nevada, but then my uncles went back to Ireland for a visit, and got married. When they returned with their brides, my dad felt like a third wheel, so he had his brothers buy him out. He left and worked in the oil fields in California before working his way down to southern California, where he met my mom at an Irish get-together.

My mom, Bridget, was a little thing, 5-foot-2 at the most. She had come over from Ireland to work for a family, and they had moved from New York to Chicago and eventually to Los Angeles. She was quite a bit younger than my dad, who was 52 when I was born. She had a tremendous personality and a great sense of humor, and when I think back about it, all of my buddies in high school were more likely coming to listen to her stories, than to see me.

My dad had all of this terrific education and spoke eight languages, while I don't think my mom went past the third grade, but she had unbelievable common sense and a tremendous feeling about people. She could spot a phony very quickly. She was a friend to everybody and didn't have an enemy in the world. All she cared about were her two sons, and ensuring that we were going to have an opportunity in life greater than what she had.

That was why she was so adamant about telling my dad that I should have the chance to play football.

The "B" team was made up of freshmen, sophomores and a few juniors. The coach saw me playing catch and told me, "You're my quarterback." The coach never showed me a play or a playbook. He would call the play in the huddle, and then after we got to the line of scrimmage, the center would hike the ball to me. Our basic play was for me to take the ball from center and turn and see who looked like he wanted the ball and give it to him. If nobody was there, I tried to take it myself and get as many yards as I could. Of course, this did not go well. The coach thought I was fouling things up, so he demoted me to the second team, then the third, then the fourth. Pretty soon I was just sitting around watching practice and the game. I did have a companion, a sophomore, who was pretty much in the same boat. Later, that friend, Norm Nygaard, would become the leading rusher in San Diego State history at that time and is now in their athletic Hall of Fame.

After college, both of us were drafted by the Los Angeles Rams, and neither of us played a down our freshman year in high school.

Luckily for me, and the rest of the team, the school changed varsity coaches before my sophomore year, and the new coach, Buzz Bemoll, turned out to be one of the most influential people in my life, along with my basketball coach, Doc Sooter. They were a major reason why I went into coaching. God bless Buzz, he's gone now, but Doc is still kicking, 82 years old now, and just a wonderful man.

Buzz had been in the Marines in World War II and had seen action in the South Pacific. He arrived with all his vim and vigor and he got us going. He was a vibrant, enthusiastic and caring man.

In his first meeting with all of us—and remember I was a skinny little redhead who had not played a down as a freshman—he made it very clear that everybody was getting a fresh start. That darn well got me going. I went right back to that Bernie Bierman book and decided I was going to be a tight end.

By the start of my sophomore year I was playing on the second team on the varsity and playing a lot. Coach Bemoll was a taskmaster, but at the same time he had a great way about him that he made everyone feel special. I'd have run through a brick wall for the man.

In later years the two of us became close friends. We shared a lot of memories and had a lot of fun on the golf course.

Coach Bemoll was going to cut a kid, a starter, from our team because he got caught smoking, which was against the team rules. The coach came to me and asked what I thought, and I never hesitated. "The kid's gone," I said. I really think the coach wanted to debate it, but I was so strong in my statement, he didn't bother. He did have the kid stick around for another day of practice, and he put him opposite me. I knew why he did that, he wanted me to really work him over, and that's exactly what I did. He left that day a really beaten individual.

One thing about high school football—it's true about professional football as well—is that the players are human and they are going to make mistakes. I have made my share. We lost a game that year that I will never forget. I was the first guy downfield on a punt return, and instead of just making a nice safe play, I decided I was going to clean the punt returner's clock, make a big play, and knock the ball loose. I missed the tackle when the guy made a good move, and I went flying by him. He took it all the way and we lost the game.

I cried all the way home and couldn't sleep all night or all weekend. When I got to school on Monday and went to practice, Coach told me to go out and lead the guys in calisthenics. He said he had a few more things to get done before practice and would be out in a few minutes.

I started yelling when I got on the field for everybody to line up and get going, and almost everybody did. I was the captain, so I think the other players looked at me as one of the leaders of the team. We had three or four players, however, who were lollygagging, and that made me mad. I stopped right there and starting yelling at them.

"Hold it right there," I yelled and started pointing fingers at them. "You, you, you and you, if you don't want to be out here, get off the field right now. We lost a game Friday night and this is BS." Three of the kids were starters. I can't imagine what would have happened if Coach Bemoll had walked out right then and seen three of his starters walking off the field. I don't know if he would have backed me up or not, but I think he would have. Luckily they all said, "Yeah you're right," and we got on with practice. One of the kids was a sophomore, and years later he came up to me at a reunion and thanked me for chewing him out. He said he always thought about that whenever he came close to giving up on something.

We had a good team, and we made it to the semifinals of the southern California championships. I think part of the reason was because Coach instilled that pride in us to work hard and do whatever it took to be successful.

In the spring of my senior year, I was voted by the school and community as the athlete of the decade. Right before graduation, my former freshman coach came up to me and said, "If anyone had told me you would do all of these things you've done, I'd kiss their butt." You know what I wanted to say but didn't.

People tend to forget, I think, that to be a really good coach you have to be a good teacher. Some of the greatest coaches I have been around in my life or have been fortunate to watch were successful because they were such good teachers. Both Coach Bemoll and Coach Sooter definitely fell into that category.

One example came during spring football my junior year, when Doc Sooter came up to me one day and said, "Jim, here is what we are going to do next year. I want to make sure you understand your role." This was during football practice, months away from the start of basketball season. He said, "You're going to play on their top offensive guy and shut him down. You're going to hit the boards. That's your deal." I looked up at him and said, "Coach, can't I take a shot?" He said, "Did you hear me, this is your game, football, and I'm telling you what you need to do for the basketball team." That's how advanced in coaching he was. That was in 1950.

In southern California, Doc Sooter is regarded as the best high school coach ever, and with good reason.

I had the great fortune of playing for him for three years. My senior year he was called back into the service during the Korean War. At that time, our team was regarded as the second best in southern California. Who knows what would have happened if he had been with us.

The big redheaded coach had piercing blue eyes, and did he instill discipline. He had several opportunities to leave the high school, but he never did. He loved where he was and was loved in return. John Wooden really wanted to hire him to be his assistant at UCLA, and he would have done a great job, but Doc decided to stay at the high school level.

I can't say enough about Coach Bemoll and Coach Sooter. Through the years, I think they knew my feelings.

Years later I really upset a lady in St. Louis one time. She was a society reporter and was interviewing Joe Sullivan, the general manager of the Cardinals, and me during a program at a downtown department store. She wanted to know who the truly outstanding teachers were when I was in high school.

"I can answer that, I don't even need to think about it," I said. "My football coach and my basketball coach."

She had this dazed look on her face, and I knew why. She had thought I would say my math teacher or my English teacher or my Latin teacher, but she had never expected I would say my coaches. She looked like she needed more of an explanation, so I continued.

"The English teacher, the math teacher, nobody ever pushes them," I said. "They don't have to go out there on the field or the court. They really should have competitions every Friday night for the English department to go against the other high school English departments, for the math departments to go against other math departments. And if they fail, and the other school's math department wins, the teacher should get fired. That's what happens to the football and basketball coaches."

She put that in her article in the paper, and a bunch of the high school coaches around St. Louis saw it and called to thank me. They know what I know—a coach can be the nicest guy in the world, but he had still better win if he wants to keep his job.

I'm sure there are high school coaches all over the country like Coach Bemoll and Coach Sooter, and I hope their players appreciate them.

In the summer, Coach Sooter would have the gym open from approximately 6 p.m. to 11 p.m. every night. He'd have leagues formed for different age groups, and all the kids in the area would come to the gym to play or practice. Coach was there every night and nobody paid him. He did it for the love of the game.

I can think of many times in the summer when we would pile into some old jalopies and drive to a neighboring town for a game. After the game we would always stop at a Dairy Queen or a similar place and he would buy everybody milkshakes, root beer floats, whatever we wanted. None of us had any money, and I don't think he had much more.

In the summer between my junior and senior years in high school, we were undefeated and won two league championships the same night at our school gym. Near the end of the first game, a player on the other team and I had an encounter. The officials stepped in and prevented us from going at one another. This guy also played football, and we were scheduled to play them in the opening game in the fall, just a few weeks away.

Coach Sooter called us over to the bench after the game and told us to go to the locker room, shower, then lay down and rest because we would be playing again in an hour. He was looking right at me when he said, "I do not want any of you to get into any altercations with that team (the one we had just played)."

That was easier said than done. As we left the gym and walked across the street to the locker room, which was next to the football field, the losing team, and my antagonist, were standing there. Words were spoken, and the next thing I knew, that fellow and I were exchanging blows.

I can still remember thinking, as the fight was taking place, this had to end quickly, or Coach Sooter would find me. Luckily I finished him off pretty quickly.

We got to the locker room, took our showers and laid down. Coach Sooter walked into the room, looked at us and left without saying a word. Coach Bemoll then came into the room and walked right over to me. He leaned down and said, "Great going, you kicked his ass. That's worth two touchdowns in our opener next season." All I can remember thinking is that I hoped Coach Bemoll left before Coach Sooter got back, and that he would not tell him about the fight.

Later I found out the two of them knew about the whole thing and had decided on their course of action. We then went out and won the second game and another league championship.

It would have been great if Doc could have been coaching us for that senior season. He had coached the team to a level where he was going to see rewards for his hard work, devotion and perseverance.

The great thing for him was that when he did come back from Korea, he became the dean of high school basketball in southern California. He produced teams and players that were second to none. He sent a lot of players on to major college basketball, including two who joined Wooden at UCLA and won a national championship.

College recruiting was a lot less regulated in the 1950s than it is now, and I was offered all kinds of deals if I would agree to go to certain schools. I was offered money and cars and other incentives. Schools often tried to pressure you into choosing them. There was even one guy who wanted to be my agent, telling me he would get me the best deal.

My dad had gotten into football a little more by then, but one thing that really bothered me was when I got the phone call that I had been selected for the All-Southern California team, he never congratulated me. My mom did, and my brother did, my coaches did, my friends did, but he never did. It really hurt me, and it stayed with me for a long time. That was really the big honor for high school players in southern California.

A few years later, I was receiving some honors while I was in college, and my dad wanted to talk with me about this game or that game. It took time for me to become friends with him, a long time, but finally I came to understand all that he had had to go through in his life. I thought as smart as he was, he should have been more than a chicken rancher. He could have been the president of a university or the CEO of a major company. I had a difficult time in a philosophy class, because I knew my dad was more knowledgeable than the professor. I didn't really appreciate the fact my dad had worked very hard to get where he was. He made the most of the opportunities he had when he came to this country, but he never had a fraction of the opportunities I received.

One of those opportunities was the chance to get a free college education in exchange for playing football, and I was lucky enough to be recruited by many very good schools.

I was walking across the high school campus one day and I saw two big guys in a good-looking car acting mysteriously. I thought they were looking for trouble. They saw me looking at them and they stopped the car. "Hey, can you help us?" one of them said.

"What do you need?" I asked. "They said, "We're looking for a kid here, Jim Hanifan."

I said, "Well, you're looking right at him." "We need to talk to you," they said, "How about getting in the car with us?"

If somebody said that to a kid today, he ought to turn around and run as fast as he can. But I was naïve, and it was 1950, so I said OK, and got in the back seat while they were in the front.

They introduced themselves, and I recognized both names. They were both San Francisco 49er players, and graduates of a certain university. I was thrilled to meet them.

They knew I was being recruited by their school, and they had come to warn me not to go there. They said they had gotten screwed over by this school, and they had heard I was pretty good and didn't want what had happened to them to happen to me. Whether that would have happened or not, we'll never know, because I listened to them. Were they good guys or not? I think so.

I was being recruited by all of the West Coast schools and the service academies. My first visit was to UCLA, and the coach there was Red Sanders. The first time I met him, he said, "OK, Jim, let's shake hands, you're coming." It made me nervous. I shook his hand, then got to school on Monday and asked Coach

Bemoll, "Does this mean I have to go to UCLA?" He started laughing.

I also went to USC, then to Stanford. That trip was the first time I was ever on an airplane, and I didn't know I was supposed to yawn or something to pop my ears. The head coach, Chuck Taylor, drove up from Palo Alto to get me, and he talked the whole way back to school, but I couldn't hear him. I just kept nodding my head.

When I went to the University of California, however, there was no question that was where I was going to go. They had been to the Rose Bowl four years in a row, and I took an immediate liking to the coach, Pappy Waldorf. The only thing he told me was that I was the first legitimate tight end they had recruited, and I knew that was the case, so that told me he was honest, and I respected and appreciated that.

I was riding a pretty good high when I got there for the first day of practice. We had a high school all-star game the weekend before, and I happened to intercept a pass and run it back for the winning touchdown. It was just a case of being in the right place at the right time.

I got to Cal and started out on what seemed like the 32nd string, on team P or something. I had to work my way up. On our first big scrimmage that fall, I kept getting selected to stay on the field and play with the next team. I was out there all day, and they wouldn't let us have water. I was standing on the sideline sucking on a towel, while the guys I had started playing with that morning were up in the stands, sitting down having a Coke or eating ice cream. I was so tired I couldn't see straight, and then the varsity defensive end coach, Eggs Manske, called upon me. He said, "Jimmy, I want you to go in now and kick some ass." Well, they drilled me. And of course, when the coaches were studying the film, they didn't take into account that I had played probably two full games already!

Lying in bed that night, I couldn't help but think about all of the glowing things they had said while they were recruiting me, how I was going to be an All-American. I was like the 32nd end. How was I going to make All-America if I was the 32nd guy on my own team? A heck of a lot of work had to be done!

I cannot talk about football people, particularly regarding Cal, without bringing up Eggs Manske. Most current football fans will not recognize his name, but he was one of the brightest people I have ever met in my life, one of the best looking and toughest men I have ever encountered. Along with Pappy, I was mesmerized by this man.

Pappy Waldorf was the Cal head coach, and he also turned out to be a very important person in my life. I really found him to be a father figure, and he was a real gentleman and a man who really cared about his players. He taught all of his players not only about football, but about life, and I think everybody who ever played for him was a better man for that experience.

A great example of how all of Pappy's former players feel about him is the organization Pappy's Boys. Some former players formed the group, named in his honor and dedicated to his beliefs. The organization is made up of individuals who were players, managers, ball boys, etc., who came into contact with Pappy while he was at Cal.

There is a statue of Pappy on the Cal campus, one of only two statues of a coach that exist in college football. One is of Knute Rockne on Notre Dame's campus, the other is Pappy on the campus in Berkeley. The statue is located in faculty glade, which shows the distinguished Cal faculty loved and admired him, too.

Pappy had taken the team to four straight Rose Bowls, and everybody in the coaching profession had tremendous respect and admiration for him, as well as genuine affection. He had an unusual gift about him. He was his own man. He really, truly cared about everybody. He cared about his staff, his players, his fellow faculty members. I think he had very few enemies in his life. To me he *was* the University of California, he was like the symbol for the whole university, in my opinion.

In the four years I played for him, I can only remember one time in practice or in a game where he raised his voice in anger or used profanity. When I was a freshman, in our game against Southern Cal, one of their linebackers tackled our star running back and then twisted his knee and tore the ligaments. Pappy came running down the sideline, calling the guy an SOB and other things, and yelling at the officials for not doing anything about it. Here I was, a baby, loving it.

By the next year, my sophomore season, I was starting at defensive end because I had broken my thumb the night before the season opener. We came into the USC game with both teams undefeated, and they were expecting a crowd of 102,000 people at the Coliseum, which was the biggest in the Coliseum's history at that time. Pappy was a great speaker with a deep voice, and the night before the game, when he got up to speak at our team meeting, you couldn't hear another sound in the room.

He said, "Gentlemen, tomorrow we are going into the Coliseum, and I don't want you to be nervous. It's just another game." Somebody snickered, and we all broke up. He started laughing too, and he told everybody to go hit the sack. That was his big pregame speech that year.

It was the only night in my life I needed sleeping pills. I knew there was no way I was going to sleep, I was so worked up about the game. It was a hell of a game, too, but we lost 10-0. It started us on a bad stretch. We lost to UCLA the next week, then went on to lose at Washington.

That same year we flew back East for a big game. Those flights took much longer than they do today because we had to stop for refueling. As I sat in my seat and looked around the plane, I noticed almost all of the other seats were now occupied. One of the few open seats was next to me.

About that time, who stepped on the plane but Dr. Glen Seaborg, our faculty representative and a Nobel Prize scientist. He was the first chairman of the Atomic Energy Commission.

I watched as he approached, thinking, "Oh no, he's going to sit next to me. What are we going to talk about for the next six hours?" He made me very relaxed by directing the conversation, asking me about my position on the team, the game itself, our game plan, etc.

I'll never forget what a wonderful man he was and how he turned what could have been a nightmare for a youngster into an enjoyable experience. Even more so, Dr. Seaborg and his lovely wife remained my friends for life.

I played both ways my junior and senior years, and while I enjoyed some individual success, we had some tough years as a team. We went 5-4-1 when I was a junior and were 5-5 my senior year. I was able to make some All-Conference and All-America teams, and as a senior I was lucky enough to lead the country in receiving. I caught 44 passes for 569 yards and scored seven touchdowns.

Our quarterback that year was Paul Larson, and he was a great football player. Not too long ago I had a chance to watch some films of Paul in action, and I had to call him up to tell him I remembered he was good, but not that good. He had no protection from the offensive line, and coaches at that time really didn't know how to teach pass protection and didn't work on it at all. The problem Paul had was despite his success as a quarterback, he really didn't have a set position. He could have been a very good running back in the NFL and enjoyed a long career, if a couple of things had broken a different way.

When you look back years later on individuals, and wonder why things worked out the way they did, it's amazing how one injury or one incident can affect their lives and the lives of others far into the future.

We really didn't have much of a passing game until my junior year, when a high school coach joined our staff, Jim Sutherland. He came out of Santa Monica High School, which has produced a lot of great football players over the years. It was a package deal, because he brought one of those players, Ronnie Knox, with him to Cal.

Ronnie was a superbly talented football player. If his old man had not fouled him up, everybody in the country even today would know who Ronnie Knox was. That's how good a player he was and could have been. We spent some time together working on our campus jobs, and I think he would have been OK with everything, if not for his dad.

We were playing our intrasquad game at the end of my junior season, and Pappy split up all of the regulars on the two teams. Ronnie was completing his freshman year, and I ended up on his team. He had a good game, and I caught a couple of touchdown passes from him, and everybody was pretty excited about his potential. He was likely going to be the backup quarterback the next year, but he had really put on a great show.

After the game, his father, Harvey Knox, walked into the coaches office and said to our backfield coach, "Well, I guess you see now what you're going to have to do, you're going to have to start my son."

That really ticked off the backfield coach, who stared back at Harvey and said, "As long as I'm here, your son will never start." That was the end of Ronnie at Cal, and it really changed the direction of his life.

His dad transferred him to UCLA, where he had to sit out a year. He made All-Coast as a tailback as a senior and got drafted by the Chicago Bears. Of all the teams that Ronnie could have gone to, the Bears probably were the worst team for him. His dad was like oil and vinegar with George Halas, the old man and boss of the Bears. Harvey Knox came walking into Chicago trying to tell Halas how his son was going to do this and that to make the Bears a championship team, and Halas took one look at him and told him to take a flying leap.

Off Ronnie went to Canada, and he really tore that league up, being named the MVP and earning other awards. He was playing in Toronto, the same team I had played for, but I was off in the service by that time. When I got home from the service and flipped on the television, there was Ronnie, starring on this weekly show. He was a handsome guy, and I guess his dad thought he could be an actor, too.

Without any warning, Ronnie just walked off the field one day and quit football. He had gotten serious with a young lady, and the two of them took off and went to Mexico. Every once in a while you would hear something about him. I got a message one day that he had called when I was the head coach of the Cardinals, but I was in a meeting and didn't get the call. He didn't say what he wanted, didn't leave a number and didn't call back. I have always felt bad about that. I heard he ended up living in Los Angeles and was homeless when he died a few years ago. I thought the world of him, and it hurts to see him gone.

If Ronnie had stayed at Cal it would not only have impacted his future, but Paul Larson's as well. The other development that affected Paul was an injury to Sam Williams.

Going into our junior years, Sam was all set to be our starting quarterback, and Paul was our halfback. Sam was on the verge of becoming the first black quarterback at a major university. He had been the backup the year before and had made All-Coast as a defensive back.

In the final scrimmage of the preseason, I'll be darned if Sam didn't get hit and separate his shoulder. This was on Saturday, a week before our season opener, and we had lost our starting quarterback.

By Monday, six days before the opener, the coaches had moved Paul from running back to quarterback. He started that week, and all he did was become an All-America selection, quite a feat.

Paul was a great athlete, extremely quick and a darn tough guy. But he truly was not a quarterback. When he went to the pros, they tried to play him at quarterback, and he never was able to have much success.

If Sam had not gotten hurt, Paul would have stayed at running back and likely would have gone to the pros as a running back and had a wonderful career. Sam came back as a senior, but Paul was already set at quarterback, so Sam switched to running back. Both of those guys ended up at Fort Ord with me, Paul playing quarterback and Sam running back.

I have been able to stay in touch with both guys over the years. Paul is living in his hometown of Turlock, California, where he has a ranch with cattle and horses. Sam became a lawyer for a big firm in Los Angeles, and for a long time was the right-hand man for longtime mayor Tom Bradley, a tremendous person who passed away much too soon. He was the president of the state legislature as well.

It was my dream to play pro football, and like everybody, I thought I would be good enough to make it. In the 1950s, however, there was a lot less opportunity than there is today. There were only12 teams in the NFL, and nine more in Canada. That was the sum of professional football in those days, and the salaries weren't too great, either.

After the season, I was selected to play in numerous post-season games, including the Hula Bowl, East-West Shrine game and the College All-Star game. That was really the honor that everybody wanted—it was almost more important to be selected for that game than it was to play in the pros.

While we were practicing for the East-West Game I received my first lesson in dealing with the media. It was not a pleasant one.

Pappy was coaching the west squad, and because we were coming off a couple of lean years, he was starting to catch some heat. Some of the guys on the team were upset because we had a practice scheduled for Christmas Eve, and they wanted me to talk to Pappy to see if he would agree to change it.

Before I had a chance to talk to him, I got a message that a reporter from a Bay Area newspaper wanted to talk to me. He was a little cigar-chewing guy. Everybody called him Greasy Ed. When I called him back, he said he had heard there were some players on our team upset about how hard and long the practices had been. I told him he was wrong, but then he said he had heard I was going to talk to Pappy about it. He asked me "off the record" what was going on.

I told him, "OK, Ed, off the record, I'm going to meet with Pappy tomorrow about the Christmas Eve practice."

The next morning, I went downstairs for breakfast and Matt Hazeltine, my teammate at Cal, a great player and a good friend who later played 14 years for the 49ers, was sitting there. He said, "Oh, you're having a meeting with Pappy, huh." I looked at him like I didn't know what he was talking about, and he tossed me a copy of the green sheet, the sports section of the *San Francisco Chronicle*. There was the headline "Hanifan to meet with Waldorf."

I almost died. I didn't have but a minute to think about it before Pappy came walking into the room. He always had an awesome presence about him, and that was true on this morning as well. He had always talked to us about the press, and said to remember whatever they said about you to take with a grain of salt.

He walked right up to me and said, "Jim, I'd like to talk with you about this." I looked up at him and said, "Pappy, Coach, don't ever believe what you read in the papers." It was the only thing I could think of to say. He knew what I thought of him, and that I would go to the wall for him, so I think that was a point in my favor. He just told all of the fellows, "Gentlemen, we will be having a meeting in a half hour."

At the meeting he said it had come to his attention that some of the players were upset about the practices and especially the practice on Christmas Eve. He said, "We are going to practice. Those of you who don't want to be here can leave. It is an honor to be here, gentlemen. You don't have to be here. We're playing for these little kids, it's not about you. If you don't like it, get out of here." Nobody left.

I was glad Pappy took the whole incident so well, and it really taught me a valuable lesson about the press. There really is no such thing as off the record. Don't be dumb. If you don't want it said or carried around, don't say it. The other person can't help it. You put the thought in his head. What amazes me is to see players or coaches meeting with the press and having interviews, and then they get all upset by what they read in the papers the next day. I have seen head coaches come into meetings ticked off because of something that was in the paper. The coach is blaming his staff for making the statement, and he was the one who said it.

I was able to earn my degree in four years, while I was playing varsity football, and this was before the days of tutors and study halls for the athletes and all that stuff they have today. I had a lot of options open to me, but I really wasn't certain what I wanted to do.

I thought about so many areas—medicine, psychology, education—but nothing seemed to be the right fit.

Coach Waldorf called me in one day after my senior season and asked me what I was thinking about doing. I told him I was interested in going to law school. He set up a meeting for me with some influential alumni, then took me to meet the dean of the Boalt Law School, which is one of the most prestigious law schools in the country. I was accepted into the school, which was a great honor.

At the same time, we had a couple of freshmen tight ends coming along, and Pappy asked me to work with them during spring ball. After spring practice, he told me he would like to add me to his coaching staff for the next season.

In that year, I had been drafted by the Los Angeles Rams, so I also had the option of playing pro ball. My choices were to go to law school, join Pappy's staff or play pro ball. It was not like I sat around and mulled it over. It took me maybe five minutes to decide I was going to play football.

CHAPTER 2

In the Army

Professional football was much different in 1955 than it is today. There were only 12 teams, with 33 players on a team, and you really were out there playing because you loved the game, not for the money.

I was drafted by the Los Angeles Rams and signed a contract for $7,000 with a $500 bonus, but I got cut before the season started. I was the last player cut.

I actually laid awake in bed at night, wondering whether if I paid them they would let me play on the team. The Rams were a very talented team, and at my position, tight end, they only had two future Hall of Famers, Elroy Hirsch and Tom Fears, along with two speedsters, Bob Boyd—the fastest man in the NFL— and Woodley Lewis, an outstanding kick and punt returner.

If I had been willing to wait, I might have hooked on with another team, like San Francisco, but when I got an offer from Toronto in the Canadian Football League, off I went. I actually got a better deal than I had with the Rams—making $13,000. I had a pretty good life going. I played that season in Canada, and soon after that season, I got a nice letter from Uncle Sam. The Korean War had just ended, and I had been able to avoid getting drafted because of school, but sooner or later, Uncle Sam was going to get me. I didn't mind serving my country, but I was upset because of the money I was going to be losing along with the chance to play pro football for the next two years.

As it turned out, getting drafted might have been one of the luckiest things that ever happened to me. I was assigned to basic training at Ford Ord, California, and they had just hired a successful civilian coach to take over the football team—Don Coryell.

Service football at the time was very popular in this country. All of the branches of the military had teams at all of their bases, and it was a real competition between the services and the bases to see who was the best. Most of the guys who were there had played college football, and several had also spent a year or two in pro ball.

The Army knew your background and whether you were a football player or not. They weren't too worried about soccer or volleyball players. But if you were a football player, they wanted to make certain you were on one of their teams.

My first impressions of Coach Coryell were that he was very intense and high-spirited. He wasn't much older than most of the players, maybe eight or nine years, but he had already been coaching for several years. He had been a high school coach in Hawaii, and the coach at the University of British Columbia, before becoming a junior college coach in Washington state. He thought it rained too much up there, so he started looking for a new job. He found out the Army was looking for a coach at Fort Ord, and he applied and got the job. He had been in the service during World War II as a paratrooper.

Don didn't care who was who, or where you had played college ball, or if you had played in the pros. He was cutting guys left and right, because he didn't think they could help his team. He was cutting guys who had been All-Americans and All-Conference. That was how good this level of football was.

In the first few weeks of practice, I was just trying to play the way I had at California and in the pros and hoped it was good enough to allow me to make the team. I guess I might have been a little over-aggressive, because one day this fellow took me aside after practice and said, "You've got to ease up." I looked at him, not understanding what he was talking about, and he said, "We're in here for two years. We're making $75 a month. Relax—don't hurt someone and don't get yourself hurt."

It was during this time that I met Bing Bordier, who remains one of my closest friends in the world.

Bing had been a tight end and linebacker at Southern Cal, and he was a great player. He came in after practice one day and said, "I'm in trouble, he's going to cut me."

"What are you talking about?" I asked him.

He said that Coryell was going to cut him, so he was going to change positions. He did, too, becoming our starting nose tackle. He still did a great job. The next year, when we were playing in Europe, he became the starting fullback and made the All-European team.

Bing had been drafted by the Redskins, but had grown tired of playing football—until he got to Fort Ord. Playing for a guy like Coryell and our coach in Europe, Cofield, was one of the reasons it was fun for him and the rest of us.

Somehow, even though he ticked off a lot of guys, Coryell's enthusiasm was able to bring that team together. We were only making $75 a month, so he had to be a really good motivator to keep us playing and winning.

We had a lot of talent, guys like Bordier, and the other starting receiver, A.D. Williams, who played with Green Bay and Cleveland. Charlie Hardy played for the Oakland Raiders and Merrill Flatley with the 49ers. Mel Hammack played for the Cardinals, Ordel Braase started at defensive end for the Colts and Sam "First Down" Brown played at UCLA, etc. It helped Coryell that there were so many good players on the team, because he basically was the only coach. He had another guy who was supposed to help him, but he didn't show up all the time.

Coryell was a real innovator, even for that time, and he was coming up with unique offensive formations, like the stacked I, that nobody had ever seen before. We were much more advanced than most of the teams we played, and we usually won fairly easily.

One time we were tied at halftime in a game against Hamilton Air Force Base. As we came off the field to go to the locker room, a scout for the British Columbia Lions, Vic Lindskog, stopped A.D. and me. A.D. was a great player. He had played at the University of Pacific and went on to play at Cleveland and Green Bay. God bless him, he just passed away a couple of years ago.

Vic started talking to us about signing with him when we got out of the Army in a year. While we were talking, he asked if we wanted a cigarette. We were in our football uniforms, but we said yeah and lit up the cigarettes. By this time Coryell and the rest of the team was in the locker room, but we were still standing outside, talking to Lindskog.

Coryell was making his halftime talk, and all of a sudden he realized his two starting tight ends weren't in the room. "Where's Hanifan and Williams?" he yelled. One of the guys said he thought we were still outside, so here he came storming out of the door and found us standing there, casually smoking and talking to Lindskog.

He spewed forth some profanity and A.D. and I both knew we were in trouble. "Get those damned cigarettes out of your mouths and get your butts back in the locker room." He really chewed us out.

We got back in the room, and then he really lost it. He went absolutely ape. He kicked a trash can and threw things all over the place. We sat there and watched him go crazy. It was a small room, with two benches directly across from each other, so we were looking each other in the eye, and it was all we could do to not burst out laughing. I don't know what Don would have done if anybody had started to laugh. It was really a fantastic performance.

The way the stadium at Fort Ord was built, our locker room was right next to the ladies rest room. During halftime, some of the wives of the generals and the other officers had gone in to use the restroom. The walls were so thin, they couldn't help but hear Don's tirade and all of the curse words he was shouting.

All of a sudden, we heard this knock on the door and a full-bird colonel entered the room. Coryell had his back to him, and the colonel belted out, "Knock off the profanity!" Coryell was in kind of a crouch, and he slowly turned around and said, "Who said that?" just as he saw the colonel standing there.

The guy was like 6-foot-5 or 6, and as Don turned around, he found himself looking right up at the colonel. "I said it," he said. You've never seen a man backtrack so fast. "I'm sorry," Don said. We were all dying, we were laughing so hard. It was too much.

We went back on the field and proceeded to kick the tar out of Hamilton. We were all laughing so hard, and none of those guys had any idea what was going on. Don still swears this never happened, but it did.

What Don didn't know was about a week later a couple of us got summoned to an investigation. It turned out some of the brass thought Don was being too abusive to the team and wanted him checked out. They asked if we were being abused, and we all backed Don. "What are you talking about?" we said. "Are you kidding me? He's a great coach. We deserved to get our butts chewed out." That was the end of that.

Don also had a soft side to him. We had a road game against Camp Pendleton, down near San Diego, and he let me and some of the other men who were from southern California drive down on our own. Everybody else was taking a bus. We were undefeated, and so were the Camp Pendleton Marines. They had loaded up their team, shipping players out from Quantico, etc.

We had a good time on our way there, and by the time we got to the base where we were staying and found our barracks, it was about two in the morning. We walked in, and there was only one person there—Coryell.

He jumped out of bed and started ripping into me and the others. I said, "Coach, where are the rest of the guys?"

He said, "I gave them the bus." I said, "Where did they go on the bus?" He said, "Tijuana."

I said, "Oh no, you didn't let them go to Tijuana." We're talking 30 or 40 men. I just knew they were going to get arrested, that we weren't going to see them again. It was dangerous down there.

Miraculously, about 5 a.m., they all showed up. They had had no incidents or problems. I couldn't believe it. Luckily we had another day before the game, so everybody was able to rest up and we went out and won big. We went on to win the national championship in service ball that year.

We all thought we had a pretty good thing going, and that we would be together the next year to defend our championship. It didn't happen though, mainly because of a man known to be a troublemaker in his own sport, baseball—Billy Martin.

Billy had been assigned to Fort Ord when he was drafted into the Army, and the cadres there couldn't stand him. He was very obnoxious and continued to be that way throughout his life. The worst thing you could do there was say you knew him. The best thing you could say is that you had never met him and didn't know anything about him. The guys in charge were so sick of him that they got him shipped out of there, and sent him to Fort Carson, Colorado.

When Billy got to Fort Carson, he raised a real stink about what was going on at Fort Ord. Basically he was charging that certain persons there were getting special privileges, and he was basically upset because he wasn't getting the same treatment. He had enough pull because of his baseball connections that he was able to get an investigation started, and it led to the downfall of football and other sports at Fort Ord. A general lost a star over it, and it also had a ripple effect on a lot of other military bases around the country.

A lot of us still had a year to go before we could get out of the service, and the brass decided we were all going to Germany. They told us that we would still be together playing football over there, but it didn't work out that way.

The worst part about going to Germany was the trip to get there. The army decided it would be less expensive if we made the trip to Europe by ship instead of flying to New York and then taking a ship across the Atlantic. So we left Monterey, went down the California coast, along the coast of Mexico, through the Panama Canal, and across the Atlantic to Europe. I think there were about 14 football players who had this opportunity to spend 19 days on a troop ship, and that gave us time to think about Billy Martin. Bing was not one of the guys who came over on the ship. He stayed behind at Fort Ord in a cozy job, living off the base, until somehow that got fouled up, and he found himself on the way to Germany to join us.

We had just reached the Atlantic, it was at the end of January or the beginning of February, when we were stuck in the worst storm I have ever been in in my life. It was so bad, you weren't even scared, because you knew it was over. It was only going to be a question of how long you could tread water. It was like we were a matchstick in the middle of the bathtub.

But somehow, God blessed that ship and that crew, and we survived that storm and made it to Germany.

We had been told that we would all be together, on the same team, living in a nice hotel in Berlin and would give Europe the finest exhibition of football it had ever seen. We were all pretty excited now that we were actually there. Before we got settled, however, the generals of all the different divisions got together and said we couldn't all go to one spot, we had to be split up, or it wouldn't be fair.

I was in the group that got assigned to the 86th Infantry, 10th mountain division, stationed in Schweinfurt, and the coach turned out to be another man who remains one of my dearest friends in the world, Colonel Pappy Cofield.

Pappy was a great motivator. He was a captain at that time and later became a full colonel. He had a lot of the same characteristics as General George Patton. He started out in the Marine Corps as a private in World War II but got an instant battlefield commission when his squad was pinned down during a fight in the south Pacific. He told the squad, "Cover me, I'm going up the hill and take them out." He took out two Japanese machine gun nests. Even to this day he won't talk about it, I found out about it from other people.

Pappy would come into the locker room before our games dressed like Patton, all the way down to his big black leather boots and swagger stick. "OK, gentlemen, here is what we are going to do." He was very organized and he developed great camaraderie on that team, much like we had under Coryell the year before. We didn't have as talented a team, and there were other teams in Europe that probably had better players, but we were able to win the championship.

When Bing left Fort Ord for Germany, he thought he had a nice gig lined up to work in the ski patrol in the swiss Alps. When Cofield found out about it, however, he got him reassigned to our base. I was happy to see Bing, but I don't think he was too happy about it. Bing thought he was going to spend the year skiing in the Swiss Alps before Pappy got hold of him. The two of them still argue about it every time they get together.

We had great support from the other soldiers at our base. In Europe, the service teams were the only football available. We were the high school, college and pro teams all rolled into one.

The regiment put on great bonfires for us the night before the games, including some where the men dressed up like girls to serve as cheerleaders. The regimental band even played in front of our barracks as we were getting on the bus to leave for games.

We also had great medical attention. A young captain, Dr. Robert Hines, was our team physician. He went overboard taking care of us. Later we found out he would bet heavily on the games. Seeing how we won the European championship, he did rather well. Dr. Hines now lives in Ohio and has done such great service to his community that the municipal stadium is called Robert Hines Stadium.

The general looked to us as his guys, and he thought our great season had a lot to do with things going so well among his troops. Morale was high, the efficency reports were good, and he thought everybody was in an upbeat mood because the football team was doing so well.

I've seen it since, as well, especially at the high school level. A good football season gets everybody excited, and the effect can carry over and last throughout the entire school year.

After we won the European championship, in 1957, all the soldiers chipped in enough money to send the entire team to Garmisch for a 10-day vacation.

As we were about to leave to return to our base, Pappy Cofield called me, Bing, and two other fellows in for a cup of coffee. He said he had something special for us, and pulled out 4 pieces of paper. It was another 10-day pass, his thanks for the work we had done on the football field. We all looked at each other and knew exactly where we were going—Copenhagen. We weren't disappointed.

Don, Bing, Pappy, Dr. Hines and I have remained friends ever since those days, and it's funny, I was so upset when I was drafted, but I ended up meeting four of the best friends I have ever had in my life. When my stint in the Army was over, it was almost hard to leave, but I knew I wasn't saying goodbye to them forever. I have often used this episode in my life to explain to a young person that what you think at the time is just terrible might actually turn out to be a blessing in disguise.

My plans were to go back to Canada and continue my career. What I didn't know was that those plans were about to change.

Don Coryell and Colonel Leaton "Pappy" Cofield talk about their friend, Jim Hanifan.

Jim is a real special person. We first met when I was a civilian and was the athletic director and football coach at Fort Ord, right at end of the Korean War. I had my choice of 16 new guys to be on the team, and Jim was one of the 16 I picked. He turned out to be a great one. He was a hell of a player even though most people think of him as a coach. He didn't have great speed, but he was such an athlete that he could catch anything near him. He was tough, playing tight end or wide receiver, and in one game he had to play defensive end and did well. He would do anything to win.

We drifted apart when he went into coaching, although I knew what he was doing. When he got fired along with the rest of the staff at California and we had an opening at San Diego State, I got in touch with him. I always hired guys I really liked who were good people, and Jim fit right in. He became the offensive line coach and did a great job. He helped guys become better players. We had a great staff, and we all got along well. He was so respected by all of his players.

If you ever walk into a convention or a cocktail party and he is there, you will know exactly where he is because there will be a big crowd of guys huddled around him. He will be holding court and everybody will be laughing. I remember walking by his meeting rooms and everybody would be laughing and talking. They were a real group and were very close.

They would do anything they could to get the job done, and that was because of Jim. He could take a bunch of guys who were tough and skilled and teach them how to be great players.

I remember after he went back to St. Louis as head coach from San Diego, we went there to play the Cardinals and they beat us. I didn't feel bad about it; they really played well. I wanted to win, but after the game, a bunch of guys rushed over to say hello. They were happy, and I was real proud of him. Somebody asked me why I wasn't bitter because I had come back to St. Louis and lost. I said it was because of Jim.

He's really something special.

— Don Coryell

I took a great football team to Germany from Fort Riley, Kansas in 1955-56, but we lost in the semifinals of the European championships both years. All but two of those players left after that second season, and all I had coming in were Jim Hanifan and Bing Bordier.

Our quarterback had been a cheerleader at the Citadel. We only had about 18 or 20 players and never played more than 15. It was amazing, but we pulled it together and won the championship. Jim had that determination and the ability to make everybody do better. I remember in one game we had a guard who jumped offsides a couple of times. Jim grabbed him and said, "If you jump offsides again I'm kicking you out of this game." He didn't say he was going to ask the coach to kick him out of the game—he was going to kick him out.

After we won the championship, all of the reporters were there wanting to know how we had beaten all of these great teams and won. Jim was sitting there and he said, "It took a lot of determination." He looked at me and said, "I told you, Pappy, we had a hell of a job to do even to win two games. You did it." It was very touching to me.

Jim was a great player and went on to be a great coach. We have been great friends ever since our time together in Germany.

— Colonel Leaton "Pappy" Cofield

CHAPTER 3

Becoming a Coach

In the back of my mind, I suppose, I expected to become a coach some day. I really wasn't prepared to begin that when I got out of the army. I planned to go back to Canada and play, maybe think about the NFL, then decide what I wanted to do with the rest of my life.

Those plans changed when I was cut by Ottawa in 1959 and found myself back in my wife Mariana's hometown of Marysville, California, about 50 miles northwest of Sacramento. I was a 26-year-old man who needed to support his family. Luckily Mariana had graduated from nursing school at Stanford and was able to get a position, but I still needed to work.

Even though I had graduated from the University of California, I did not have the hours of education classes I needed to become a teacher and coach at the high school level. I decided what I was going to have to do was take a position teaching at a junior high school and work on getting the classes I needed to get a high school credential.

Talk about being scared. I was more nervous that first day of school than anytime I ever stepped on a football field. I had all these books, and it was all I could do to stay one step ahead of the kids. My salary for the year was $4,020. It was worth it to me, because I knew I wanted to coach and teach, and it was a step I had to complete to get where I wanted to go.

Luckily Mariana was supportive of me or it might have been more difficult. She was also understanding about my always stopping by the local junior college after school to watch the football team practice. Bud Van Beren was the head coach, and he had played at Cal several years before me. I knew of him, and he knew of me. He thought I was still playing and didn't realize that I was now teaching in the area.

My first break into coaching came when one of his assistants who handled the offensive and defensive lines had a heart attack. Bud had found out by then that I was living in the area, and he called me and asked if I would be interested in helping out. I jumped at the chance, even after I found out it was a volunteer position. I spent all that extra time at practices, in meetings and at the games for the next three years and never got a penny for it.

The experience I got was invaluable, however. Bud is a wonderful man, and he really was embarrassed that he couldn't pay me. He was a great coach who spent many years later as the coach and athletic director at Humboldt State and we have remained good friends.

The lessons I learned about coaching in those three years were incredibly important to me later. I was just like all players—I thought I knew everything there was to know about the game, but I found out how wrong I was. One of the youngsters—and remember they were only seven or eight years younger than me— would ask, "What do I do on this play?" or some other question, and many times I had to say, "Wait a minute, I'll go ask Bud and find out."

I also was getting quite an education teaching at that junior high. Some of those teachers couldn't figure me out, especially the older ladies. They actually asked me, "Jim, I can't understand why you are even here. Why are you here?" I told them I had to do it to get the teaching certificate I needed to move up to the high school. I also was commuting to Sacramento State to fulfill the requirement. When I got the certificate, I was really happy, because now the door was open for me to become a high school football coach.

I wanted to move back to southern California, and when I heard through the grapevine about a school having a possible opening, I sent in my application. A couple of schools near Marysville talked to me about jobs, but I really had my heart set on going back to the southern part of the state. Maybe I was brainwashed as a player, but I honestly thought the programs in southern California were superior to those in the northern part of the state.

I lined up a couple of interviews and drove down, wondering what was going to happen. One of the interviews was in my home town of Covina, but not at my old high school. The other was at a big-time football program at a high school in Pasadena.

That Pasadena interview was one of the scariest things I have ever been through. It was like I was applying to be the head coach at a college. They had faculty members and players on the team there to interview me. It was a predominately black high school, and it seemed like many of the questions were about how I would handle this racial issue or that racial issue. I had never thought about it, so I didn't have any prepared answers. I had to say what came to my mind and what I thought. I didn't know if it was what they wanted to hear or not.

The other interview, at Charter Oak High School, went much more smoothly and they offered me the job. I had to sign a letter of intent, which I did, and I was excited to get back home and tell Mariana.

When I walked in the door, she said, "The superintendent of schools from Pasadena just called and offered you the job." I didn't know what to do. The Pasadena school had a lot of great kids and a very good team coming back for the next season, but I had already given my commitment to Charter Oak. I called around and asked some people I respected for their advice, and finally decided that since I had given Charter Oak my word even without a contract, I had to take that job. I turned down the Pasadena job. I have often wondered what would have happened had I accepted it, but that is one of life's mysteries that will never be answered. I now had become a head high school coach in 1962.

I know I made the right decision. The coach who took the job at Pasadena stayed a couple of years, moved up to a junior college and then was forced out of coaching. I got to be around some great kids at Charter Oak, and many of them have stayed in touch with me over the years. We actually had a reunion in 2002 when the Rams played at Denver. It was the first time I had seen many of them since high school. They presented me with a scrapbook one of them had put together, including letters from a lot of the fellows, and it is something I truly treasure.

It wasn't like I knew I had made the right decision immediately, though. We started out the year by losing our first four games. I said to myself after that fourth loss, "Well, we've answered one question, you can't coach. Now what are you going to do, Jimmy boy?"

What we did was turn it around when the kids started playing better, and we were much improved in the second half of the season and actually finished second in the league. We only had 22 players on the varsity, so each one was special to me.

One day, I asked one of the players to stick around after practice and run through some extra drills. Walking back to the locker room, this player asked me why I was picking on him. "Son, when I stop picking on you is when you need to worry," I said.

Especially coaching at the high school level, I know I relied on the experiences and lessons I learned from Coach Bemoll and Coach Sooter in dealing with my players. I wanted these kids to know how much I enjoyed coaching them, and how much I wanted them to be successful, not just in football but in school and in life.

In the letter he included in that scrapbook, Steve DeThomas, our quarterback, wrote, "He taught us football as a four-star general would his troops. I remember when he handed me a book that was half the size of the new Sears catalog. It was our playbook. He told me I would be fined $5 if I lost it."

The other change in coaching at the high school level was I actually was being paid to coach—an extra $600 tagged on to my teaching salary. I had a junior class in U.S. history, a sophomore class in world history, and a senior class in civics. They were all enjoyable, except I couldn't believe it when I picked up the textbook we were supposed to use for the civics class. It was the same book we had when I took the class in high school. It was boring then, and it was still boring.

I went to the principal, Rudy Duvanich, and said, "I have to talk to you about this book. It's an absolutely boring book. Why do we have to use this?" I suggested a book I had just finished reading, *The Making of the President, 1960*. I told him that book explained everything, was interesting, and that the kids would really get something out of it. The principal told me if I could get every kid in the class to buy the book, we could use it.

I think the book cost $2.50. The next day in class I really did a great sales job. I opened up the standard civics book and talked about how boring it would be, then said I was going to give them an option. I said if each of them would buy the other book, we could use it and have a lot of fun, but if even one kid resisted, it was back to the old, boring gray book. Then I asked for a show of hands. That put a lot of pressure on them, but every kid agreed. I guarantee those kids learned more by reading that book than any other civics class in the country that year. Before I go any further. I have to say I had two great people who helped me immeasurably, Rudy Duvanich, the principal, and Sam Cipriano, vice principal. We remained friends throughout their lives.

Some people in the area must have thought I had done a good job coaching, because I got some feelers about some other coaching jobs at the end of the year, including from some junior colleges. Juco football in southern California is very big. It definitely was a step up for a coach to move to juco from high school, and many people were surprised when I turned all of them down.

I told them my reasons were simple—my kids. I said, "If I leave these guys now, they are never going to believe another word a grownup says. I would be the biggest phony in the world."

Those kids really were special to me. We had one player who broke his nose in practice on a Thursday, the day before our game. He was my quarterback and linebacker. When we took him to the hospital, the doctor asked him what position he played. He said he was the quarterback, and the doctor told him he could play. He started the next night at linebacker and played the entire game. He knew if he had told the doctor he played linebacker he would not have let him play, thinking he would get hurt making tackles. I was privileged to be around those types of young men.

At the end of my second year at Charter Oak, I again got some inquires from junior colleges. I made the decision that what I really wanted to do was become a coach at the college level, and to do that I probably needed some experience at a junior college. Becoming a college coach was going to be my ultimate goal, or I might have stayed right there at Charter Oak.

As it was, I moved on to Glendale City College and stayed for two years. That was when I got another break, accepting a job to become an assistant coach at the University of Utah. My former teammate at Cal, Mike Giddings, had become the head football coach and I went with him.

This level of football obviously was much different, especially when it came to recruiting. We were going after a different caliber of player than we had recruited at the junior college level, and I quickly found out there was a direct correlation between how good a recruiter you were and how good a team you were going to be able to put on the field. We had a very good coaching staff: Tom Louat, Chuck Banker, Jim Criner and I went onto the NFL. Ken Vierra, who left coaching and went into private business, could have been the best of all of us.

One weekend we brought in a kid who we thought had the chance to be a pretty good player. He just did everything he could possibly do wrong the entire weekend. Most times if you are a good football player, you can get away with stuff, but I just didn't think this kid was going to work out.

At the end of the weekend, I drove him back to the airport, and when we got there I told him, "Here's what I want you to do. I want you to go to one of those other schools that is recruiting you. After this weekend, and how you've acted, I've come to the realization that I would have your sorry butt here for the next four years and that I would have to put up with you, and I don't need it. No thanks. There's no harm done. You go your way, and I'll go mine. Good luck to you."

I got back in the car and drove home, and I started laughing. I knew I couldn't let the head coach know what I had just done, so I knew when it was announced the kid was going to another school I would have to say, "Jeez, no coach, I don't know why we lost him. That other school must have bought him off or something, gosh dang it."

A couple of hours after I got home, the phone rang, and Mariana answered it. She called to me downstairs, "It's Dale Nosworth, that high school All-American wide receiver, who was just up here, from Long Beach." I'm thinking, why in the world is he calling me? I just told him off. I answered, "Yeah, what's up?"

He said, "Coach, I had a chance to think about things on the flight back to LA, and I've made my decision." I said, "Yeah, where are you going?" like I really gave a rat's rear end.

He says, "I'm going with you."

"What?" I said.

"Coach, the more I thought about it, I need you. You were absolutely right, I was a horse's rear end. I need you to keep me under control. I want to come to Utah," he said.

I said, "Well, since you put it that way, I think we can work that out."

I got off the phone and thought, I've got a new recruiting gimmick. Then the next time I tried that on a prospect, he told me to stick it.

It really wasn't a gimmick with this kid, however. I meant it. It turned out that I coached him for three years. He started out as a wide receiver, but he was too slow, so I moved him to tight end. He developed into an All-Conference player.

He was really upset when I got a chance to go back to my alma mater, Cal, as an assistant coach. I told him I had done everything I could for him, but that if he really wanted to play at the next level, in pro ball, he had to move two more spots inside, to guard, because he was too slow even to be a tight end in the pros. He wouldn't do it, but then he called me about three years later and said, "Do you think it's too late?"

Cal had fallen on some hard times in the 1960s. They had gone through the free speech movement, etc., so it had been difficult to keep a top-flight athletic program going.

My old roommate, Ray Willsey, was the head coach. He asked me to come back and assist him, and I thought the situation was brighter at Cal than it had been in some time. I thought it would be a good move. Ray did a terrific coaching job under the most trying of times. I truly believe he is responsible for football still being at the University of California.

I never will forget one day in 1971, not too long after the students were killed at Kent State, and violence was erupting on college campuses all across the country. The chancellor of the university, Dr. Roger Heyns, came to practice that day and spoke to the team. "You are the last group of the establishment," he said. "You're it. Thank you very much for withstanding all of the problems." It was a tremendous tribute to Ray and to the players. It gave each coach a sense of pride. Maybe we were holding everything together.

One night Ray and I were having dinner near the campus, and I looked out the window. All these people were walking by in orange gowns carrying what looked like tambourines and chanting. "Ray, what's going on?" I asked. He said, "Don't worry about it." They were Hare Krishnas, and they were all over our campus.

The next year, we were doing a great job recruiting, getting a lot of the top high school and junior college kids in the state to come to Cal. We also had beaten our in-state conference rivals, Stanford, UCLA and USC, the previous season.

We had a big blue-chip weekend planned, bringing in the top 30 kids in the state with their parents. We had sessions with all of our Nobel Prize winners and a lot of dignitaries, including famous alums. But guess who was having a big get-together the same weekend—the Hare Krishnas. There must have been 1,000 of them or more, right by our campus, in their orange gunny sacks. We got all of these state cars to transport the kids and their moms and dads around, and we must have driven three miles out of the way so they would avoid seeing the Hare Krishnas. We were saying, "It really is a short trip to the stadium, but we're going to take the scenic route."

Alas, the NCAA decided our staff had committed some recruiting violations, and the entire staff was fired. Whether you were innocent or not, you were included.

Even though I was extremely upset about what had happened at Cal, it turned out to be one of the best things that ever happened to me.

I had remained in touch with Don Coryell, who had gone to Whittier College after he left Fort Ord, and then had become the coach at San Diego State. What I didn't know is that he had been watching me, and I had developed a pretty good reputation as a recruiter with some of the kids I was able to get from southern California to come to Utah and Cal. He told me, "I'm tired of recruiting against you and want you on my side."

I also had a chance at that time to go back to Canada and be an assistant coach with the Edmonton Eskimos, but I really wanted to work with Don, so I accepted that position. The only reason I could see myself leaving San Diego State was if the head coaching job at Utah opened up. Otherwise I thought I would stay in San Diego forever.

When we were talking, it never even came up about what position I would coach. All the way back to juco, I had been working with quarterbacks and receivers, so I thought I probably would end up with one of those jobs. Then I found out he already had both of those coaches, so I really had no idea what I was going to do.

Don and I were in the car one day, going to pick up some furniture, and I asked him, "By the way, what am I going to be coaching?" He said, "The offensive line."

I almost had a heart attack. I had not coached the offensive line since being a head coach in high school. I put up a mild protest, but Don insisted that I could do it. That's how I became an offensive line coach.

It was not totally new to me, since I had been involved with the offensive line meetings as a player when I was a tight end, and obviously had coached all phases of the game at high school. At this level, however, we needed to be much more sophisticated in what we were trying to do. I had to study my tail off, trying to learn as much as I could and formulate my own ideas about what I thought was a good strategy and what I thought would work. I also had a young grad assistant, Ray Ogas, to help me. He had just finished playing offensive line at San Diego State.

One of the things I have always liked, respected and admired about Don is that when he hires an assistant coach, he pretty much gives him free rein to coach his area. A lot of head coaches supposedly give their assistants that responsibility, but don't give them the total freedom to coach the way they see fit. Don was the ultimate in allowing his assistants to coach.

Don had great faith in his coaching staff. He basically told me, "You are the head coach for the offensive line. If you want to do something and you think it will work, do it."

One of the things Don did at San Diego State was come up with the different numbers for different types of pass plays. Two would be a slant, three was an out, four was a square in, etc. Everybody uses that system today, and it was Don who came up with it. There are so many ways Don Coryell changed or influenced offensive football that it would stagger a person's mind. He definitely should be in the NFL Hall of Fame.

We had a great season, 10-1, and played Iowa State in the predecessor to the Holiday Bowl. We whipped up on them 30-0! The staff was looking forward to some time off, and I was planning to drive up to Utah and visit some friends. When I went into Don's office to talk to him before I left, he looked at me and said, "You know what we ought to do?"

I looked at him and had no idea where he was going with this. He continued, "The two of us should coach pro football."

I just stared at him. "Well, do you want me to buy the team or are you going to buy the team," I said.

He said, "No, I'm serious, we ought to be doing that."

After spending those few days in Utah, I was back in southern California recruiting, and I was riding in the car on the San Diego Freeway with Rod Dowhower, who was our quarterbacks coach. We had the radio on, and the announcer came on and said, "This news has just come in over the wires. The St. Louis Cardinals have hired Don Coryell as their new head coach."

Both Rod and I couldn't believe it. I'm surprised we didn't drive off the road. We headed straight to the campus, and by the time we got there, everybody was going crazy. We had a message from Don to call him. When we did, he said he wanted us to join him with the Cardinals.

I had applied for the job as the head coach at Nevada-Las Vegas, and Rod had decided he was going to go with me if I got the job. Another one of the assistants, Claude Gilbert, wanted to become head coach at San Diego State. Claude deservingly got the head coaching position, and Ernie Zampese stayed with him at San Diego State.

I really thought I was going to get the Las Vegas job. The chairman of the board of regents basically told me I had the job, but later in the day, while I was talking with a vice president about trying to get more money for the assistant coaches, he said they had not made a decision about the head coaching job. I smelled a rat and called Rod and said forget about Las Vegas, we're not going there.

Where we were going was to St. Louis and the NFL.

CHAPTER 4

Welcome to the NFL

The move to the Cardinals and the NFL had happened so quickly that I didn't really have time to be nervous. There also was a bit of a comfort factor built in, because I knew I would be working for Don, and Rod also was going to be on the staff, and even though it was something I never really thought about, the challenge was an exciting one.

The Cardinals had not been very good in 1972, going 4-9-1 under Bob Holloway, which was the reason he and his staff had been fired. They had to win their last two games of the season just to get their record to that level.

I really had no idea what kind of players we had, and I really wasn't even sure what my job was going to be. I knew Rod was going to coach the quarterbacks, and Don was bringing in another young college coach, Joe Gibbs, to be the running backs coach. Joe was coaching at Arkansas but he had played and worked as a graduate assistant for Don at San Diego State before I got there. I thought I was probably going to be the receivers coach.

We wanted to become as familiar with the returning personnel as possible, so we tried to watch as much film as we could. I was in the film room one day, only a few days into my new job, when one of the Cardinals' players came into the offices to introduce himself. It was Jackie Smith, the tight end.

I had never met Smith, but it turned out he knew about me. One of my teammates in the army had been a teammate of his in Louisiana, and Smith said he talked about me all the time. Coryell was in a meeting when Smith came by, and Jackie asked who he was talking to. It turned out it was the fellow who had been the offensive line coach the year before.

"If he hires him, I'm retiring," Smith said.

When Don's office door opened, I shot in there. "Did you hire that guy?" I asked. Don said no, and then wanted to know why I was asking.

I told him what Smith, who had to be one of our best returning players, had said. Then I said, "I've been looking at all this film, and I've got to tell you, I can do twice the job that's been done here. Let me coach the offensive line. Give me a year, and if I don't get the job done, fire me."

He said, "You're right."

The Cardinals' owner, Bill Bidwill, had tried to tell Don the one assistant coach he wanted him to hire who needed to have professional experience was the offensive line coach. That might have been true, except that we were throwing the ball at San Diego State more than almost everybody in pro ball. I could tell from watching the Cardinals' linemen on film that they had never been taught the proper mechanics of pass protection.

Bidwill was taking a chance by hiring a college coach, but I think he had a good feeling about Don. He had his scouts check him out pretty thoroughly, and he knew Don had won at whatever level he had coached. The other thing I think Bill liked about Don was that Don was very unassuming. He didn't want or need all of the media attention to massage his ego. He didn't want a radio show or a television show, and he didn't want to be a big-time public figure. That made Bill feel good, because he is very uncomfortable being in the public eye as well.

I could tell from watching the films that we had some good players, but they were not being used in the proper way. Dan Dierdorf was moving around at different spots, Tom Banks was playing guard, Bob Young and Conrad Dobler were backups. The other thing I could tell immediately was that none of them knew how to pass block.

We had developed a different style of blocking at San Diego State, where we had our linemen striking the defensive linemen, instead of having their arms up with their elbows out. When a guy like Deacon Jones saw a lineman trying to block him that way, all he had to do was give the guy a head slap, and he could run right past him.

This new technique in pass blocking was foreign to the NFL and really to all of football, except for San Diego State. We started perfecting it and going through all the pros and cons of it. I truly believed in it and was convinced that this was the way to go.

When we arrived in the NFL in 1973, the basic technique for an offensive lineman in pass blocking was to assume a hitting position with his arms up and place his hands on the defensive lineman's chest. His elbows would splay out; an absolute dream position for a defensive lineman. The offensive lineman would assume a passive position on the defender and would hope to buy enough time for the quarterback to get the ball thrown. He would put his body in front of the defender like a sacrificial lamb.

There also was a rule in the NFL stating than an offensive lineman could not extend or lock out his arms on a defender. Over the next two or three years, I had some heated discussions with officials and, in particular, Art McNally—the head of officials on this rule. I would ask Art to think back to when he was a kid and got into a fight. "Did you remember not to extend your arms?" Obviously, he got the point. You can't do it!

So the first thing I told those Cardinal linemen was that we were not going to be passive in any manner. In pass protection we were going to strike and stop the defenders in their tracks! Chill"em!

The fellows took to it and started enjoying pass protection. Once in a while an official would call us for unnecessary roughness for locking out (straightening out) their arms as they struck a defensive man. We lived with it! Finally at a league meeting, the head coaches and owners abolished the defensive man's ability to head-slap (a violent arm swipe to the side of the head). Don Coryell came back after the league meetings and said "Well, you did it." I said, "What?" He then went on to tell me about the abolishment of the head-slap but that the whole thing had been brought up about the St. Louis offensive line using their hands and violently striking the pass rushers.

Supposedly with the abolishing of the head-slap, we now couldn't strike.

Well, when that hit the papers my offensive linemen came storming into my office screaming about it. I told them to relax. The hand is quicker than the eye and we are not changing anything. Obviously this method of pass protection has continued on through the years and I'm very proud to have been the guy who developed it and brought it to the NFL in 1973.

At our first mini-camp, I brought all of the linemen together and showed them what I wanted, how we were going to change the way they were used to blocking. I also got their attention right away by bringing up something I saw in the newspapers, that George Allen, who was coaching the Washington Redskins then, had called them the worst offensive line in the league.

That made them mad, which was the reaction I expected. "I know you are mad, and I don't blame you," I said. "But here's the deal. What are we going to do about it? If this guy thinks this, I'll bet there are other guys out there who think the same thing. We have a tremendous challenge here. Here's what we're going to do."

Approaching it in that manner turned the negative into a positive, and gave us a goal. It also helped them listen to my ideas. The first day, when we got out on the field, I took Dan aside and showed him the footwork he needed, and what he should do with his hands. He looked at me and went, "Really?"

"Hasn't anybody ever taught you this?" I said, knowing he was a second-round draft choice from a big football power, Michigan. I told him to try it and see what happened. He did, and finished his opponent off. He looked back at me, and I'll never forget the look that was in his eye. It was as if the mystery had been solved. Thank you.

The only member of the line who really had any stature at the time was Ernie McMillan, who had been to four Pro Bowls. After the last practice of the mini-camp, Ernie came up to me and asked if I was in a hurry to go anyplace. I said, no, not really. He said the fellows were going to go to a particular place and have a couple of beers and they would like for me to join them.

"Thank you," I said, "I'd like to do that."

The entire offensive line was there, and Ernie handed me this little plaque they had made. It said, "One for all, all for one."

"We have the feeling you are that kind of guy," McMillan said. "We haven't had that kind of coach around here."

After just three days together, this was a real sign that the players were accepting me, and I knew if I could develop that confidence between the players and myself we would have a much easier time doing what we needed to do to be successful on the field. They also had seen that some of the changes in their technique I had suggested were working, and that gave them a little more confidence about me as well.

The coaching staff also was working together very well. Joe Gibbs fit in immediately with Don, Rod and I, and that was the extent of the offensive coaches. It wasn't like today where you have maybe twice that many coaches for each side of the ball, plus special teams. It was just the four of us. Because we were such good friends, it really didn't seem like work when we put in such long hours.

An interesting thing happened that first spring in St. Louis! Don, Joe and I were in the office on Memorial Day, and because it was a holiday weekend, we were the only ones there. Joe and Don had been in the office for a while when I showed up, and Joe came up to me, exasperated.

"It's your turn to take care of him, I've been with him all morning," Gibbs said. Already a big car racing fan, he was anxious to leave so he could go watch the Indianapolis 500.

"What's the problem?" I asked Joe.

"He's in the bathroom, but he hasn't been able to go to the bathroom. His bowels are stuck, and he won't let me call the doctor."

As Gibbs started to leave, I walked into the bathroom and heard Don grunting and groaning.

"Coach, what's the problem?" I said to Coryell.

He explained it to me, and I said I knew what was happening because my daughter Kathy had had the same problem when she was a baby. I told him her intestines had gotten wrapped up wrong, and we were able to get her to the hospital and get everything straightened out.

"What would have happened if she had not gone to the hospital?" Coryell asked.

"She'd have died," I said.

When I said I thought we should go to Barnes Hospital, Coryell agreed. I called the team doctor, Dr. Bernie Garfinkel, and he said he would meet us at Barnes.

As we walked past where Gibbs was watching the race, I told him we were going to Barnes. Gibbs wanted to know how I had persuaded Coryell to agree to go.

"It was simple," I said, "I used the one word that really motivates people—death."

When we got to the hospital, the doctors got Don all fixed up. When they let Joe and me see him, he was as white as the sheet covering him. "Congratulations, it's a boy," I said. He didn't think that was funny.

Training camp that year was at Illinois State, in Bloomington, Illinois and I had another idea I wanted to throw at the offensive linemen to see how they responded. At San Diego State, one of the things we had done was in our goal-line offense, I had the linemen get down in a four-point stance instead of the traditional three-point stance. A lineman's goal at that point is to get underneath the defensive player, and if he is already in a four-point stance to your three, he is going to be lower than you. It used to drive me crazy as a player when a coach would yell out to get lower, drive that guy off the ball. The guy's head was already on the ground, there was nothing I could possibly do to get lower than him. All I could do was to get on top of him.

I went through this one day at training camp, showing them how I wanted them to do it, and Tom Banks was the one with the biggest reaction. "Well I'll be Goll-darned," Banks said. "Jim, that's the most intelligent thing I've ever heard a football coach talk about. I wonder why we've never done that. We didn't do it at Auburn, and we haven't done it here. That's a pretty good idea."

It didn't take me long to realize that while we had some good offensive linemen, we had to make some changes in order to maximize their ability. Dan had been playing some at left tackle and some at guard, and I just sensed he was a natural right tackle. That was where Ernie had been playing, obviously with a great deal of success, so I was a little nervous when I went up to him and said I had an idea I wanted to talk with him about. I asked him what he would think about moving to left tackle, which I thought he could handle, so Dan could switch to right tackle. I asked him to think about it, and he said, "I don't need to think about it, I can give you my answer right now. Sure, I'll do it." It was a great gesture on his part, and was the first step toward making our offensive line so good.

The other move I wanted to make was to move Tom Banks from guard to center. He was good as a guard, but he was a natural-born center. One of our backup guards the year before had been Conrad Dobler, who had been cut and then re-signed, and I made him a starter.

We won our first two games, but then fell into a bad stretch, losing four in a row. Our next game was at home against the New York Giants, a team we definitely thought we could beat. We knew we needed this win to break that losing streak and to stop some of the negative talk that was beginning to develop around the stadium and the city.

Walking from a meeting room to the practice field on Friday, two days before the game, our game plan fell out of my back pocket. Dierdorf saw it, and he knew it was mine. It contained all of the blocking schemes for the game against the Giants.

Now Dan could have just called out to me and said, "Hey Jim, this fell out of your pocket," but no, that would have been too easy. He saw a great opportunity to play a joke on me, and he immediately enlisted the aid of some of the other players.

I, of course, had no idea the game plan had fallen out of my pocket. When I looked for it later and couldn't find it, I started to panic. I looked in my locker, I looked in my office, everywhere I could think of. The last thing I wanted to do was to tell Coryell that I had lost the game plan.

This had happened Friday afternoon. Saturday morning we had our normal walk through and light practice. I again searched all over the place looking for that damn game plan.

As we finished up the practice, Don called for all of the players to gather round him for some additional thoughts about the game.

When Don finished talking, Jackie Smith stepped up and said, "Coach, my good friend Jack Gregory (the All-Pro defensive end of the Giants) called me last night and said they have our game plan."

Don just about flipped out, as did several of our players, especially Larry Stallings, one of our linebackers. It had come to this.

I felt terrible. I had let everybody down. I stepped in front of Don and the squad and told them it was me—I had lost the game plan. Tears were streaming down my cheeks.

With that, the whole team broke into laughter, including Don. Dierdorf and Smith had gotten all of them in on the joke, including the head coach. There I stood, realizing I had been had. I went from despair to joy in one quick moment. The even better news was that we beat the Giants the next day.

I also was in on my share of pranks, like the time we got Wayne Sevier, a young coach who was working with us those first years in St. Louis as kind of a graduate assistant. He had played for Don at San Diego State and wanted to be a coach and eventually was an outstanding special teams coach for a long time in the NFL.

One of the great jokes in the NFL that had been passed down for years was to tell the rookies they were going to get a free turkey on Thanksgiving. Jim Bakken had gone to the local grocery store and got some stationery and wrote up the letter about how to get your free turkey and passed it out to all of the rookies.

Wayne was the guy we really wanted to get, however. Joe Gibbs and I shared an office, and we were set to get Wayne on one particular evening. He walked down the hall and I called him into the office. I said, "Hey you know Jackie Smith has got all of our turkeys at his restaurant, and we were just wondering if you wouldn't mind running out there and getting them for us."

When Wayne said he would do it, I faked a phone call to Jackie to tell him Wayne was coming to pick up the turkeys. Don was sitting on a couch in our office, and he had to put the newspaper in front of his face so Wayne would not see how hard he was laughing.

When Wayne got there, Bakken and John Zook were sitting at the bar, and they were picking the meat off the bones of a turkey. Wayne told the bartender he was there to pick up the turkeys for Coryell, Gibbs and Hanifan.

Dierdorf and all of the other guys were sitting there, and Dan yelled out, "Waynesy baby, you're the turkey!" and everybody started laughing except Wayne.

He drove back to the stadium, and when he walked by our office I called out, "Hey Wayne, where's our turkeys?" He said, "If we lose this game Sunday, it's your fault." I told him that was a really big-time comeback.

There were a couple of additional notes which makes this an even better story. The next day after practice, Bill Simmons, our equipment manager, passed out a certificate to everyone who had been victimized, calling them a Great Turkey. Then he said, "We have a special award this year, the All-Time Greatest Turkey, and it goes to Wayne Sevier."

Wayne had to go in front of everybody and have his picture taken holding that turkey carcass that Bakken and Zook had carved out the night before.

Years later, in 1979, we were in San Diego and Wayne was with us. I got to the stadium early one Sunday and was looking at a copy of *Pro Magazine*. In it was a story on Bill Simmons and his son Danny, who also is the equipment man for the New Orleans Saints. I was reading the story and it talked about some of the funniest things Bill had seen during his years in the league, and then he said, "But the best one of all ..." was the Wayne Sevier turkey story.

Wayne comes in the room, and I told him, "Hey, there's a story about you in *Pro Magazine*. You are becoming quite the celebrity." He didn't believe me, but a little while later I caught him looking at the magazine. I was laughing, Gibbs was laughing, and then Wayne slammed the magazine down. That's one of the all-time great stories.

Going back to the early St. Louis Cardinals days, it was easy to tell right away that Dierdorf was going to be the leader of that offensive line. Not only was he a tremendously gifted football player, he had that personality and wit that made everybody else look up to him. I noticed at that first mini-camp how smart he was and how coachable he was. Those kinds of guys are always a coach's favorite players.

When we beat the Redskins that year at Busch, he grabbed me on the sidelines and said, "You were right, you were right. I didn't really believe you."

Even though we finished with the exact same record as the team had the year before, 4-9-1, I could sense things were changing. Players were becoming more comfortable in their abilities, the team chemistry was improving, and I could tell they had a lot of confidence in Don and the assistant coaches.

We, in turn, were becoming more convinced the team was going to be successful. Late that year Dan hurt his knee in practice with a blindside shot, and it didn't look like he was going to be able to play. We were facing the Bengals in Cincinnati and we didn't know if he would be able to play or not.

Before the game we wanted to see if his knee was OK, but we didn't want to do it on the field where the Bengals could see us. So we went into one of the underground concrete halls at Riverfront Stadium, and I lined up as the defensive end to go against him. He wasn't in pads, just shorts and a t-shirt.

He moved good and said his knee was fine, but then we lined up one more time. As he started to lean, I happened to hit him just right and he went flying because he didn't have any strength in the knee. I really thought I had hurt him. All of the stadium vendors were walking by wondering what these two crazy men were doing.

I asked Dan if he was hurt, and he said, "Only my pride." He said the knee didn't hurt, and he went out and played. It wasn't until the fourth quarter that his opponent took an inside charge against him. My admiration and respect grew immensely for him that day.

He went on to become one of the best offensive linemen ever to play the game. If he made one mental mistake in a game it was unusual. He was a very instinctive player, but also very smart. He really took to coaching and believed in the technique that was taught. That was all he needed. He had all of the physical tools one needs to be a great player. He was a natural "big" man, and he didn't need to do all of that work in the weight room to get up to 300 pounds. That was his natural size.

He also had the ability to get to me, and he knew it. Joe Gibbs and I spent all summer after that first season working on a different blocking scheme for our big nemesis, the Dallas Cowboys and their flex defense. As we began preparing for the game that week, I had the blocking sheets and I passed them out to the linemen as we began our meeting.

As I was passing them out, I said, "OK fellows, let me have your attention," but before I could go any further, Dan yells out, "What's this?" referring to the blocking schemes. "What do you mean?" I said.

"The blocking is totally different," he said. "The most important game of the year and you're changing the blocking pattern?"

I was ready for him. "Darn right we've changed it," I said. "I'll tell you right now, has it been good the other way? No. We're going to kick their butts. Just shut up and listen."

Dan was the guy the others would respond to, I knew that. To his credit, he listened, and we put our new scheme into action. We scored the first four times we had the ball. The blocking scheme was really driving them crazy. This was when the Cowboys had Harvey Martin, Too Tall Jones, Jethro Pugh, Randy White, just a great team.

At the end of the game, Lee Roy Jordan was going crazy screaming at the officials that our linemen were holding him. I remember Dan coming up to me on the sideline. "You were right, you were right, I can't believe it."

One thing always worried me about Dan, and that was whenever his hand went up during a team meeting. He was just like Conrad Dobler, and I knew if either of them said anything to Coryell, I was going to hear about it. I was always watching him, wondering what he was going to say, and usually saying to myself, be careful now, don't go there, oh jeez.

That is exactly what happened during one team meeting a couple of years later.

We were getting ready to play the Redskins. Like most coaches, Coryell said he never read the newspapers, but he read them like everybody does. If somebody said something bad about him, Don remembered it. It was bitterly cold that week in St. Louis, with wind chills something like 20 below zero, and we could not be on the field very long or we would freeze. Larry Wilson and George Boone went out and chipped ice off the field for a couple of hours so we could practice our red zone passing game. The forecast said it was going to be that cold for the game as well.

It just so happened that in the newspaper that week was a story about the Alaska pipeline. It talked about how hard it was to build, especially with all of the weather problems there. Don read it, and he decided he was going to use all of that information for a big time motivational speech at our meeting the night before the game.

He starts out the meeting at the hotel by talking about all of the people going up to Alaska to work on the pipeline. They were having trouble working up there because of the extremely cold weather. The people in charge were trying to figure out why these men were having so many problems withstanding the weather.

The workers were from California, Texas, etc., and they couldn't stay out in the weather. But the Eskimo, he'd stay out all day. Was it the texture of their skin that made a difference or what?

I'm sure most of the people sitting in the room were wondering where in the heck Don was going with this story, but then he made the connection.

"You know what the Redskins have been doing this week?" Don said. "They've been out in the 40- and 50-degree weather lollygagging around. We're just like the guys in Alaska, we've been out in the cold weather. Those doctors and scientists knew what the difference was with those workers in Alaska. The Eskimo was used to that weather. He had been in it his entire life. He could be out all day in the cold weather, and it wouldn't bother him.

"We've got the Redskins coming in tomorrow, and they're not ready for it. We are."

I was in the back of the room, and saw somebody raise his hand. I was hoping that it wasn't one of my group, but it was— Dierdorf. Coryell saw him and said, "Yeah Dan, what is it?"

I cringed as Dan began to talk.

"Coach, I have to ask you a question," Dierdorf said. "What do I do tomorrow if I break the huddle and come up to the line of scrimmage and there is an Eskimo lined up opposite me?"

It brought down the house. I couldn't believe it. I know a lot of head coaches who would have been ticked off, but God bless Don, he took it all in stride. People were falling off their chairs laughing, pounding the floors and the walls with their fists, and finally the room quieted down. Don said, "Well Dan, I don't think even George Allen can coach an Eskimo well enough to beat you."

As I've said, Dan became the leader of that terrific offensive line, but another guy deserves a lot of credit, too. I mentioned how McMillan agreed to move to left tackle to open a place for Dan, and even though Ernie left after the 1974 season to play for Green Bay, he really helped bring that group of linemen together.

He led by example, and all of the other youngsters saw the way he approached the game, how professional he was. That rubbed off on them.

With the knowledge they got from him, plus their own intelligence and passion for the game, there was a spark to that group. And the person who most often lit the match was Conrad Dobler.

The Cardinals had drafted Dobler out of Wyoming in 1972, but released him before the season started. When a couple of their linemen were injured early in the year, however, they re-signed him. All he needed to show what he could do was to get a chance, and it wasn't long before he got it.

We were in Mankato, Minnesota, scrimmaging against the Vikings, during the 1973 preseason. Another player was starting ahead of Conrad, but as soon as he ran on the field, he ran back to the sideline. "I don't have my mouthpiece," he said. I just said screw it and yelled for Conrad to get in there. That's how he became the starting right guard. The other guy never got back in there.

It didn't take long for Conrad to earn a reputation as the meanest man in pro football. He was on the cover of *Sports Illustrated* and they called him that. I will say this—most of the time he was legal, but barely. He just got carried away at times. He was going to win his individual battle, get his man, doing whatever it took. It wasn't always pretty, and there were an awful lot of defensive linemen around the league who hated his guts. One of them was the Hall of Famer from the Rams, Merlin Olson.

Olson was doing the *Father Murphy* television series a few years later, and they had a scene that was set in a cemetery. He had them take one of the stones and make it up like it was Dobler's, complete with a date of birth and a date for his death. The people took a picture of it, and it wound up in the *Sacramento Bee*. A friend of mine saw it and sent it to me.

That was too much. I asked our public relations department to call the people at the television show and get me a copy of the picture. They did, and I had them put a caption under the photo—the ultimate compliment to an offensive lineman—and then I gave it to Conrad.

A few years later, we were all attending a league meeting or something—Dierdorf, Dobler and I—and Olson, who had retired, was there too. Conrad wouldn't let it go. He goes, "Hey Merlin, you thought you were funny with that grave marker, huh? Well, you know where I put that photo? I put it right over my toilet, so every time I go to the bathroom I'm looking at you." I made sure we got out of there before Merlin had a chance to offer any more comebacks, or punches.

Conrad would get into fights all the time, even with his own teammates. One time in practice, he got into a fight with a young defensive tackle, Charlie Davis. It was a cold day, and Don got mad and tried to step in between them to break up the fight. One of them took another swing and hit Don right in his nose and broke it. Blood was flying everywhere, and Don was cussing up a blue streak. Some of the guys were trying very hard to keep from laughing. Later in the locker room Don was sitting there mumbling about "that Gol-darned Dobler."

After a while I really stopped worrying about Conrad getting in trouble, except it usually prompted some type of reaction from Don, directed toward me, and I was in turn supposed to chew out Conrad.

One time, a defensive lineman got spun around when he was blocked by Conrad and Tommie Banks, and his butt was directly in front of Conrad. I don't know why he did it, but Conrad hauled off and kicked him. It was very humiliating to the guy, and the umpire threw a flag and gave Conrad a 15-yard penalty.

Don saw the flag, but he had not seen what caused it. Don came running up to me on the sideline, yelling "What happened?" I said calmly, "Conrad kicked the guy in the butt." Don said,

"He did what?" I told Don again and this time he said, "Tell him not to do that."

What happened more times than not was Conrad's opponent would get so fed up and frustrated with him that he would be thinking only about getting even with Conrad and would forget all about the fact his job was to get to the quarterback or tackle the ball carrier. Guys who played against Conrad were always worried about what he was going to try to do to them, break his arm or his leg, hit him on his sore knee, whatever the case might be. All of those things combined to give Conrad a great mental edge before the game even started.

Conrad became a favorite not only of the local media but the national reporters as well, because he always said what he thought and didn't care who he offended. That drove both Coryell and me crazy. Don would come up to me and say, "Tell him not to say that."

Conrad never worried about what he said. He would say, "Yeah so and so, I don't think he's worth a darn. I'm going to kick his butt tomorrow." He usually did.

Often times Conrad would sprint down the field and make a block that was legal, but just barely, before the whistle had blown. It was always close. When I complimented him one time for such a play, one of the other linemen said to me, "Why do you do that?" He had hustled his butt down the field, giving extra effort and at the last second making a clean block. I responded, "How about you getting off your lazy butt and doing the same thing? If you do the same thing he does, I guarantee you we're going to have something going."

Conrad did that enough times that all of a sudden his buddies were doing it without even knowing they were doing it. He did it one time and knocked out Cliff Harris, the great defensive back from the Cowboys. Thank God Cliff didn't get hurt. I talked to him about that play a couple of years later and he said the only thing that bothered him about the hit was that he didn't know where he was for about 10 minutes. That hit really upset Don, even though no penalty was called. Don told me, "I don't want him doing that anymore. You go tell him." I went and told him, "That's the way to do it. That's the way to hustle down the field. Where were the rest of you guys?"

Conrad would get mad at some of his teammates, and me, upon occasion. Whenever he got mad he wouldn't talk. Players always look forward to Friday's practice, because when it is over, it is their last chance to relax before the game on Sunday. Most of our fellows liked to go sit around and have a couple of beers and unwind.

This one Friday, I really wanted them to watch a couple of more reels of film to make sure everybody knew what we had planned for Sunday. I kept pointing things out to Conrad. "Conrad do you see this, do you see that?" Conrad was mad at me, so he wouldn't talk or answer.

I kept running the film back, over and over, waiting for Conrad to tell me he saw what I was trying to point out. I counted one play—we saw it 28 straight times. Finally Dan had had enough. "Conrad, would you please answer him," Dan said. "Don't you understand what is happening? He is going to keep doing this until you say something."

Conrad finally says, "Yeah Jim, I got it." I said, "Thank you Conrad, thank you very much."

I was running the projector one time and Bobby Young got mad at Conrad for some reason. The room was dark, but here came Bobby leaping over the projector. He came down like he was a whale right on top of Conrad. You didn't want Bobby to get you in a headlock, or it would all be over. Conrad was laughing so hard he couldn't retaliate. A bunch of us had to pull Bobby off him.

I don't think any of the other players were really jealous of Conrad about all of the publicity and attention he was getting, but one time they decided they had seen enough and had to do something about it.

It was during training camp at Lindenwood. Phyllis George, who was the first woman broadcaster working in the NFL, was coming to town with her crew to do a story on Dobler. They were going to do the interview and go to lunch. Conrad had done a really good job of keeping this information secret. He knew as soon as Dierdorf or anybody else heard about it, he was going to catch a lot of flak.

The day came for Phyllis to arrive. Conrad had these soft blue denim pants that were really big back in the 1970s. He asked me how I thought they would look for the interview. I told him, "On your big fat ass, nothing is going to look good."

He also had a white shirt that was more like a blouse, and this big gold medallion he was going to wear. He really thought he was dressing to the max. I just shook my head and walked away.

We were out on the practice field when Phyllis and the crew arrived and sat down in the stands. We would have been better off canceling practice, because the whole team kept looking at her in the stands instead of concentrating on what we were supposed to be doing on the field.

Jackie Smith, Jim Bakken and all of the guys kept staring up at her. Finally practice was over and the players went back to the locker room to shower and change. The team's offices were one floor above the locker room, in one of the college's dormitories, and I was doing an interview with Phyllis there. I was answering all of her questions, and saying what a wonderful young man Conrad was, when it sounded like all hell was breaking loose below me.

When the interview ended, I went down to the locker room and couldn't believe what I saw. Lockers were all smashed in, and nobody was around. Finally I saw Bill Simmons, our equipment manager. He was almost doubled over on the floor he was laughing so hard.

"Bill, what happened?" I said.

He told me Conrad had been in taking his shower, getting ready for the interview, and came out and was combing his hair. Jackie, Dan and the rest of the guys were watching him as he put on the white shirt and gold medallion. Then Conrad realized he had forgotten to use this Pearl drop polish he had bought to try to whiten his teeth, so he got his toothbrush and returned to the bathroom.

This got Smith more than anything else. He could not stand it any longer. The big redhead went back to where Simmons was sitting and said, "Give me the shears." Simmons tried to put up a protest, but Jackie insisted, and Simmons finally gave him the cutting shears.

Smith went over to Conrad's locker and he and Dierdorf took those powder blue denim jeans and cut one leg off at the crotch. They dumped it in the wastebasket and handed the shears back to Simmons.

The way the pants were hanging on the locker, you couldn't tell from looking at them that one of the legs had been cut off. Here comes Dobler back from the bathroom, all ready to do his interview except for putting on his pants. He took them down from the locker and saw what had happened.

"My pants," he yelled out. "Somebody cut the leg off my pants. Who did this?"

Everybody told me Dobler went nuts. He grabbed this long bench that was in front of the lockers and used it like a club, smashing the lockers and everything else in his way.

"I'll kill the SOB who did this," he yelled. Everybody was scared of him anyway, but even more so now than normal. "I want to know who did this."

He went to Dierdorf and Banks and everybody else, asking who had done it, and nobody would tell him. He had to wear something else to the interview.

Going up in the air to catch a pass during my days at the University of California.

The Cal-Stanford rivalry is a great one, and it was nice to catch a pass in the big game at Stanford Stadium.

Celebrating my first win as a head coach, over the Eagles, in 1980.

One of my favorite pictures of some great warriors: Tommie Banks, Conrad Dobler and Dan Dierdorf.

My group of linemen from the Redskins, the Hogs.

Mariana and I share some good times with Benny Perrin, Curtis Greer and Roy Green.

A coach is always filled with a million thoughts.

Stressing a point to Ryan Tucker during a game.

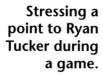

A coach is always teaching, even on the sideline during a game.

The energy level on the sideline during a game is tremendous, and I enjoy every minute of it.

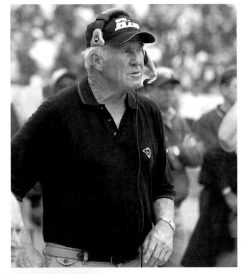

Mugging for the camera with Mike Martz after our Super Bowl win over Tennessee.

I got a chance to visit with former President Bush before the Super Bowl in New Orleans in January, 2002.

Kurt Warner and I are all smiles on the bus ride back to the hotel after winning the Super Bowl.

The night Mariana and I spent with President and Mrs. Bush at the White House after winning the Super Bowl was a great thrill.

I was honored when I was picked to be the grand marshall for the St. Patrick's Day parade and to have my picture taken with a Clydesdale.

My son Jim, son-in-law Bill and grandson Austin.

I am certain I am telling Commissioner Paul Tagliabue what he can do to solve the problems in the league.

Sharing a laugh with my good friend Joe Gibbs.

Jack Buck was a great friend, and we shared many great times together.

I have the utmost respect and admiration for my longtime coach and friend, Don Coryell.

I was honored and proud when Dan Dierdorf asked me to present him to the Hall of Fame.

Conrad Dobler, Dan Dierdorf, Tommie Banks and I shared a great weekend when Dan was inducted into the Pro Football Hall of Fame.

My daughter Kathy and son Jim.

I was happy when Dick Vermeil gave me the chance to come back to St. Louis with the Rams.

The next summer, after the rest of training camp, the entire season and the mini-camps, my family and I were planning to go to Yellowstone on vacation. Conrad and his family were living in Laramie, Wyoming, so I called him to tell him what we were doing. He said great, he would bring his family and meet us up there.

One morning the two of us decided to go fishing. It was like 6 or 6:30 in the morning, and nobody else was around. We were sitting there putting our poles in the Yellowstone River, and Conrad said calmly, "I know you know who did it."

I said, "Who did what?" He said, "You know, who cut the leg off my pants."

This was almost a full year after that had happened and Conrad had not forgotten. "I want to know who did it. I'm going to kill him," Conrad said.

"Conrad," I said, "it's been a year. Let it go. That's ridiculous for you to still be thinking about that." I lost it, and started rolling on the ground because I was laughing so hard.

We went on like this for several minutes, he insisting that I tell him who had cut his pants. I thought, "Here I am alone with this guy in Yellowstone Park and he is going to kill me." I was the only coach who knew, and I never told him. I think he figured it out over the years, but if not, he knows now. Smith could be a tough guy if he was mad at you too, and I think that was one of the reasons nobody came forward and told Conrad that Jackie and Dan had done it, or Jackie would have been all over them, too. Years later, Conrad actually gave the pants to Dan, who still has them.

For all of the things that people can say bad about Conrad, however, I don't think there was anybody on our team who didn't love him dearly and would do anything for him. He also truly epitomized the guy who got everything he could out of his ability. He is in the Missouri Sports Hall of Fame, and I really think he should be in the Pro Football Hall of Fame.

There are guys who are Hall of Famers but never got everything they could out of their ability. Conrad used everything he had from his brain power to his physical skills. He had a built-in, tremendous desire to succeed. He had his image, but there really were only a few people who truly knew him and knew what he was like. The image was that he was this tough, hard-nosed blustery guy. In truth, he has the softest heart in the world and will give you the shirt off his back. I admire and respect him a great deal and am proud to call him my friend.

One of the best compliments Conrad received came after he was traded to New Orleans. I was coaching the Pro Bowl in Hawaii and Archie Manning, the quarterback of the Saints, was there.

Archie came up to me and said he needed to talk to me about Conrad. We met after practice and Archie told me, "As much as Conrad has helped our team and me, I cannot stand to hear the pain. Every time he comes in the huddle, I hear him moaning and groaning from the terrible pain in his knees. You've got to talk to him about retiring."

Archie went on. "When we break the huddle and get to the line, I hear a collision near me, and Conrad is knocking the living hell out of somebody. It's just awesome. But I can't take it to see the pain that he is in." Archie then continued, "The Saints have tried to help me by bringing in talented wide receivers and running backs, but Conrad has helped me more than anyone!"

I told Archie, "That's one of the greatest compliments a guy can get and I'm going to tell Conrad about it. But I can't tell him to quit. Nobody can tell him that. He will know when it's time to go, when he can't take the pain any longer."

As was the case with Conrad, I honestly feel all of those guys who were there during the Cardiac Cardinal days are my friends, they are really like family to me. The other two guys who were there the longest were Tommie Banks and Bob Young.

If Bob Young had gotten started in the right direction when he was a little younger, I think he could have been a Hall of

Famer. That's how good he was. He probably was the most underrated player we had on that offensive line.

Bobby went to the University of Texas, and made the All-Southwest Conference freshman team. Texas had a really good team that year and was going to the Orange Bowl, and had a defensive lineman who was going to be the number-one draft pick in the NFL. The Texas varsity coaches told me that in those workouts before the Orange Bowl, Bobby was beating the stuffing out of that top draft pick.

If Bobby had stayed at Texas, I am sure he would have been a very high draft pick and his pro career would have started at a much higher level. But after that freshman year, he transferred to a much smaller school, Howard Payne University. I asked him about it years later, and he just told me he had a chance to go back to his hometow —and that he got a house, a car and a boat out of the deal.

He ended up getting drafted and played for Denver for a couple of years, then got traded to Houston. The Oilers cut him, and the Cardinals picked him up on a $100 waiver claim. When we finally started to work with him, I realized you really needed to prod Bobby to make him go. He had a mean streak in him, but he also had an easy-come, easy-go attitude much of the time.

Bobby wasn't that big, about six foot one, but he weighed about 280 pounds and was a big barrel of a man. He really got into the weightlifting, and won the NFL's strongest man competition and other similar contests. He went all over the world competing against a lot of weightlifters. I remember the first time I saw him I thought he looked like a well-educated banker. He had a pot belly, his hair was parted on the side, all prim and proper. That's one of my guards? You've got to be kidding me.

If Bobby didn't like the individual he was lined up against in a particular game, I knew he was going to have a big day. He also played very well whenever he knew he was going up against a very talented opponent. On days when he didn't have that motivation, his game tended to drop a little bit, and that was one thing you had to be on him about.

Nobody could question his toughness. He played a game one time with a broken hand and was wearing a cast. He decided he wasn't playing as well as he should, so he took the cast off during the game. I thought he was going to take a shot or something to at least dull the pain, but he played into the fourth quarter, didn't allow a sack and really played an outstanding game.

He came up to me on the sideline with about two minutes to go in the game and said, "Jim, how about taking me out of the game? My hand is really starting to hurt." I said, "Oh, the shot is wearing off?" And he said, "I didn't ever take a shot."

That tells you about Bobby. He was a wonderful person. He never knew how good he was or could be. He called me up one day after our first season and wanted my advice. He had been offered a college assistant coaching position in Texas for $13,000 a year and was considering taking it. I told him I thought for a starting salary that was a pretty good deal, but that I had him penciled in as the starting left guard the next season.

"Really?" he said. "You're kidding me. What about Tommie?"

I told Bobby I was moving Tommie to center, and he paused for a moment and then said, "Count me in."

After his playing career, Bobby did become a coach with the Oilers and did an outstanding job. He helped a lot of those great offensive linemen there, like Mike Munchak and Bruce Matthews. We talked all of the time about strategy and drills, problems he was having with a player, the draft, whatever was going on. He really worked hard at being a coach. I was always getting on him about trying to lose some weight because he was really heavy, and I was worried about him.

Dierdorf and his family were out visiting us at our cabin at Lake Tahoe a few years ago. I came back from playing golf and Dan came out of the cabin and told me, "Stop right there, I've got to talk to you. Something bad has happened."

He scared the daylights out of me. Then he told me: Bobby had died of a heart attack. He was only 52 years old.

Dan tried to tell me I didn't need to go to Texas for the funeral, but then Conrad called and said, "Jim, this is when Bobby needs us." So we all went and served as the pallbearers.

Bobby had been instrumental in patching up my relationship with Banks, which had deteriorated after I came back to St. Louis as the head coach. Tommie really was a great student of the game and would have been an outstanding coach. That's why the move to center was perfect for him, because he was the guy who set up everything on the line.

He was very quick and very athletic. When I came to St. Louis with Coryell he was clean cut and didn't have the Wolfman image he developed a couple of years later. He was really into electronics, and he wired my whole house for sound. I told him he ought to open a music store, but he never did.

I'm not sure how it happened but Tommie wound up with some personal problems, and when I came back to the Cardinals as the head coach, the problems affected his play and I had to let him go. It was a difficult decision, but because of it, Tommie was able to get the help he needed and now is a very happy and successful man.

We had not talked for quite a while after he was released by the Cardinals, when Bobby Young, who now was coaching the Oilers, and I were at a hospitality party at the Senior Bowl in Mobile. Tommie came over to see Bobby and really, I think, to see me. Bobby told me Tommie was there and wanted to talk to me. "Bobby," I said, "We'll do that, but there is one catch. Tommie has to apologize."

Bobby looked at me and said, "I understand. You wait right here. I'll go fetch him."

Bobby and Tommie came walking back together, and Tommie had his hand out. I did not extend my hand. He said, "Jim, I am so sorry. I sure was wrong."

When he said that, I put my hand out and grabbed him and hugged him. We both broke down and cried. We have remained close since and I think the world of him.

Two other guys who were key players on the line in those years were Roger Finnie and Keith Wortman. Roger was the guy who followed Ernie McMillan at left tackle and Keith came in a couple of years later.

Roger had been a defensive tackle with the Jets and had been traded to the Cardinals. Early in training camp we were going to release him. I said, "Hold it. Before he leaves, how about me having him for a couple of days?" Coryell said OK.

Roger came out to practice, and after half the first practice I could tell he was better than all of the other rookies and free agents I had been working with. We kept him, and after he learned how to play offense and the system, he became the starter and did a great job.

He was the only guy off that main group of Dierdorf, Dobler, Banks and Young who didn't become an All-Pro, and that has always bothered me. He always had the job of going against the defensive line's best pass rusher, defending the quarterback's blind side, and we were a team that passed the ball a lot. He always shut that guy down. I only remember him having one bad game, against Harvey Martin and the Cowboys, but the next time he won the battle.

Some of the fellows had been talking for years about getting everybody together and having a reunion, but they all said, "We can't do it without Roger." I worked for months trying to find him, going through the NFL Alumni and everything and couldn't locate him. Then one day I was at Florida A & M working out a player, and that's where Roger had gone to school. The assistant coach I was with was Alonzo Highsmith's dad, and I said to him, "One of my former players went to school here, Roger Finnie." I didn't even have a chance to say I was looking for him, what had happened to him or anything and he said, "I know Roger. I played with Roger."

It turned out he knew where he was, too, working as a minister in Florida. I finally reached him and we had a nice visit.

Keith Wortman came in and got a chance to play when Dierdorf broke his jaw. Keith had been cut by Green Bay and we picked him up near the end of the 1975 season. I liked what I saw of him, so I told the front office that off season, "Don't worry about drafting a guy; just get this guy signed." He was a little undersized, but he worked hard and put on some weight and became a very good player.

When Dan broke his jaw, our next game was against Dallas on *Monday Night Football.* Everybody assumed I was going to start a rookie, Greg Kindle, but I knew I was starting Wortman. I told Keith, but I told him not to say a word because I wanted Too Tall Jones to think all week that he was going up against this rookie, Kindle. Keith started and he played a great game, and we won it when Jim Hart hit Jackie Smith with a pass for the winning touchdown.

Having the opportunity to work with and see people like that develop, have great careers and then go on to become successful after their careers is one of the best parts of coaching. I have been really fortunate in my life to work with a lot of players like that.

That offensive line really received a lot of plaudits over the years, and they deserved it. Dan was the offensive lineman of the year four years in a row. Dan, Bobby, Conrad and Tommie were Pro Bowlers. One year we only allowed eight sacks, and the eighth was really a joke.

We were playing the Redskins and had the ball at about their 38-yard line. Jim Bakken came running on the field. It would have been like a 56-yard field goal, and Bakken—as good as he was, and I think he should be in the Hall of Fame—didn't have the leg for that. It was going to be a fake. I was on the sideline thinking, "You've got to be kidding me."

We hiked the ball and everything got all screwed up. Bakken got tackled, and that counts as a sack. The guys were mad at me, and I was like, you don't think I'm mad about it, too?

All of those offensive linemen had a passion for the game, and they were also very intelligent and very sharp. They also were sharp football-wise, and that isn't always the case.

I was fortunate to be in the right place at the right time with Don to come to St. Louis just when that team was ready to take off. We had a lot of great players in positions other than the offensive line, and it was fun to watch Jim Hart, Terry Metcalf, Mel Gray, Jim Otis, Jim Bakken, Roger Wehrli, Larry Stallings and all of the other defensive guys. I really thought we were close to becoming a championship club.

Part of the reason the players jelled so quickly, I think, was because of Don. Don was obsessed with the game. He wasn't content to be like everybody else. He was always thinking about what he could do differently, and coming up with things nobody else did. I think on top of that, it was his enthusiasm and his exuberance that really sold the kids on him and convinced them to buy into what he was saying.

One day in practice, Jackie Smith caught about a 40-yard pass. The first guy down the field to congratulate him was Coryell. He ran all the way down there. "Jackie, that was beautiful," Coryell said. I don't think Jackie had ever had a coach run down the field like that, especially a head coach. I know that sold Jackie on him. When everybody else saw his passion, they couldn't help but buy into it, too.

Don made Hart the starting quarterback. We got lucky by getting Metcalf in the draft because Coryell knew him and had tried to recruit him to San Diego State before he went to Long Beach State, and we already had Otis and Gray there. That gave us everything we needed to have an explosive offense. Coryell told me after Rod Dowhower left to go back to coach with Dick

Vermeil at UCLA that Hart wanted me to become the quarterback coach.

That is usually the one position as an assistant that gets noticed by the media, and I knew the move would help me on my career quest to be a head coach. But I felt loyalty to my guys on the offensive line, so I told Don I appreciated the offer, but I was going to keep doing what I was doing.

After getting things started in 1973, we took off the next year and went 10-4 and won the division title but lost to Minnesota in the first round of the playoffs. We were even better in 1975, going 11-3, but once again we got beat in the opening playoff game, at Los Angeles against the Rams. I really wish we had been able to play one of those games at home; it might have made the difference.

In the 1976 preseason, we took a trip to Japan to play the first NFL game out of the United States. Don was determined that everyone would have a good time, so we practiced in the morning, and he ordered that all of the meetings had to be finished by 1:30 p.m. so everybody could enjoy the sights. The coaches went on some of the sightseeing trips as well, and one thing I noticed was that I didn't see any dogs or cats.

I found out the kids' pets there were these big black beetles. We were at this stand where they sold them, so I bought two beetles. I really wanted to sneak them into Ray Willsey's room, but I never got the chance. Ray was back working with us as a defensive coach.

One night, one of the beetles got loose in our room. It was about three or four in the morning, and it was circling like a helicopter and landed right on Mariana's face. She screamed, and was using my name in rather bad ways. She was so loud that the two trainers who were in the room next door came pounding on our door. "Did you kill her or she kill you?" John Omohundro said. "It's the beetle," I said. I had to hear about that for a long time.

As we were leaving for the airport, I saw a kid and gave the beetles to him. It really made his day.

We went 10-4 again in 1976, but this time missed the playoffs, and you could just tell things were starting to change. Don was getting frustrated by a lot of the problems he was having with the front office, particularly when it came to the college draft and signing free agent players.

It seems like the draft has always been a mystery for the Cardinals. Where most teams want the input and advice of their coaches about the evaluation of players, and the team's needs for the coming year, the Cardinals—at least back then—kept the two departments totally separate. All of the assistant coaches had to watch the draft from a room in a different part of the stadium. The only coach who was even allowed to be in the "war room" during the draft was Don, the head coach.

In the 1977 draft, we had a chance to draft Robin Cole, a linebacker from LSU who would have been perfect for us. He was just the player we needed. All of the assistants sitting there watching the draft couldn't believe it when he was still on the board as our turn came. We were sure we were going to take him, and everybody was very happy.

Then came the announcement. "With their first pick in the draft, the St. Louis Cardinals, select, from the University of Missouri, quarterback Steve Pisarkiewicz."

We just sat there, dumbfounded. Cole went to the Steelers and had a very long and productive career. All of the assistants got up and left the stadium. The end of an era was coming.

Of course that era really wasn't over until the 1977 season came to a close. We made one run at having another good season, winning six games in a row, but we lost the last four to finish at 7-7.

In the next-to-last game of the season, we lost to the Redskins. That was the game where Don had made his whole Saturday night speech about the Eskimos and the Alaska Pipeline. It was bitterly cold that day, and Don's wife, Aliisa, and the kids were in the stands. Some of the fans got on Don, and yelled at her, and that had not happened before. She told Don about it after the game and that really upset him.

To have some fans take out the loss of a game on his wife and children was more than Don could take. He knew he was going to leave, and he and Bill Bidwill had several conversations and confrontations.

We lost the final game of the year, at Tampa Bay, and the problems between Don and Bill did not end. The feud continued to simmer for more than a month, and it was very obvious by some of the statements that Don was making that he really wanted out. Bill eventually got to the point where he fired him.

We had joked when we all moved to St. Louis about the way the previous coach, Bob Hollway, had been fired. He showed up for work on Monday morning the day after their last game, and suddenly his key didn't work in the door. Bidwill had changed the locks.

It wasn't so funny when it happened to us. I was supposed to meet Joe Gibbs at the stadium to work out and then go to lunch. It was on a Saturday, and I was just getting ready to leave the house when the phone rang. It was Joe.

"Don't bother coming to the stadium," Joe said. "The keys don't work."

That truly was the end of an era. Don was moving back to San Diego, but it looked like he was going to be out of coaching for a little while. I had a year left on my contract, and thought I would probably be staying, even though I had no idea who Bill was going to bring in as the head coach.

Even if I had a million tries, I don't think I would have guessed right.

Joe Gibbs talks about his friend, Jim Hanifan.

Jim is a storyteller. He can start off on one story and move on to four others before he gets back to the first one. He likes to talk. I'll never forget one night when we were in the office real late and got into a big discussion. There were six of us there, and Jim always talked more than anybody. Somewhere in there he got cut off about twice. It was about 3 a.m. and he jumped up and said "I can't get a word in edgeways." We put up one of those hanging cards where you had to take a number and wait your turn to talk. If it wasn't your number you couldn't talk. He was screaming at us because other guys were talking so much.

One of the best things about Jim Hanifan to me is that he is a great people guy. You can't get mad at him. We would get in bitter arguments about something and 10 minutes later he would say, "I'm sorry about that." You never walk out of there being upset at him. He would go out of his way to help anybody with anything. He drove 20 minutes out of his way to pick up Rod Dowhower when he was coaching with us in St. Louis, and I told him,""You're an idiot."

We won the Super Bowl together, but what I remember more is all the funny things that happened late at night, more of the journey toward getting there than the actual championship. The friendships that developed were more important.

Part of being a good coach is being a good teacher and having a passion about what you are doing, That shows up when you stay in meetings that go on and on. The other part of being a good coach is having good people skills. Jim definitely had that. People believed in him. He was really sincere about what he was doing. He didn't have an enemy in his life.

He is a great friend.

— Joe Gibbs

CHAPTER 5

Bud Takes Over

How in the world Bill Bidwill got the idea to hire Bud Wilkinson as head coach of the Cardinals, I will never know. I also couldn't believe Wilkinson wanted the job. Bill actually interviewed me for the job, but I knew it was a phony interview. I knew there was no way I was getting the job.

When he hired Wilkinson, however, the football world was in shock.

Bud had been one of the greatest coaches in the history of football when he was at Oklahoma, winning national championships and setting records for consecutive game winning streaks. He had been retired for 14 years, and there must have been some reason why he thought coming to the Cardinals was a good idea.

I had heard so much about him, of course, but had never met him until he joined the Cardinals. As he was coming in, the coaching staff was in turmoil with everybody either leaving for a new job or talking about leaving. Joe and I had discussed our possibilities, but we both knew we had another year remaining on our contracts with the Cardinals.

Joe had an offer to join his old boss at USC, John McKay, as the offensive coordinator at Tampa Bay. He said, "Let me go in first, thank Bidwill, then you can go in. They don't care if I stay or go." So Joe walked in there, came out a minute later, waved goodbye and was on his way to Tampa.

Monte Clark, the head coach of the Detroit Lions, had called the Cardinals and asked for permission to talk to me. Joe Sullivan, the general manager, granted that permission, and that opened the door for everybody. I had options—at least six teams were vying for my services. I thought I was back in high school, being recruited all over again.

By this time, the Cardinals had gone back and looked at my contract and realized I was signed for another year. They said I couldn't talk to any other teams. I just laughed. They were the ones who had messed up, and I knew I was free to do whatever I wanted to do.

What I really needed, however, was advice, so I called Pete Rozelle, the commissioner of the NFL. Pete was a very powerful individual, but he also was a regular guy. I'll never forget calling him, not once or twice but several times, and each time if I didn't immediately reach him he returned the call within 15 minutes. Does that tell you about the man or what?

When I finally sat down with Bud, I told him I thought it was probably best if I left. He said that was fine, he wouldn't stand in my way. His exact words were, "I read you loud and clear." Then I went to see Bill, and he almost flipped out. I told him his head coach had given me permission to leave.

The more I thought about it, however, the more it seemed to me the best decision was to stay, so that was what I did. It was the right decision. I got to spend that year with Bud, and what a wonderful man he was. I marveled at the man because he is such a super human being. He probably has more charisma than anybody I have ever met in my life. He also was a super football coach—in college. He brought Pete Elliott up from Miami to be on the staff, and he was an absolute gem of a human being. You will never meet anybody ever who will have one bad word to say about Pete Elliott.

The problem was that Bud was miscast as a pro coach right from the beginning. He was such a brilliant man, it just was not fair to ask him to do something he wasn't prepared to do. Again, the biggest question to me was why he took the job even when Billy offered it to him. It just didn't make sense.

Bud was truly a national figure and had so many contacts in so many places. One place where he knew all of the important people was in the automobile industry. At a time when a lot of teams were having real problems getting free cars for their assistant coaches, Bud was able to get cars for everybody on our staff. Bud actually had about three cars for himself, and one was a brand new Ford LTD. We took turns driving the car, with each of the coaches getting it for a week or so then turning it over to the next coach.

My week to have the car happened to be the same week that all of the scouts from across the country were meeting in St. Louis. Bidwill threw a party, and then we were going to watch the baseball game. I had a lot of friends in town, people whom I had either played with or against or had coached with or against. After a couple of innings at the game, a bunch of us left and went around the corner to Kelly's Corner, where the owner, John McMahon, was a good friend of mine.

One of the scouts, Tom Braatz, for some reason liked the stockyards in East St. Louis and the Stockyards Bar. He decided he wanted to go there, so we all agreed to go with him.

I had never been there so I was following them in the new Ford LTD. We went across the bridge into Illinois, but then they surprised me and took the first exit. I was going too fast and couldn't make the turn, so I went on and took the next exit. When I came off the ramp, I realized I no idea where I was except that I was in downtown East St. Louis.

I knew better than to stop. I kept driving, hoping I would come across an area where I could stop and get directions. I kept driving, and pretty soon I was in the boonies, way out in the sticks. I was on a country road, and I was really lost. All of a sudden, here comes this cotton-pickin' train.

I stopped, thinking it would be maybe 30 cars or so, but no, it's one of those unbelievable Midwestern trains that can have 200 or more cars. I started to count the cars, but after about 30 or so, I got tired of that.

What I had not done was put the car into park. I still had the car in drive, with my foot on the brake. It was getting late, and after a while, my head started to drop. Pretty soon my head dropped to my chest, and my foot came off the brake. I slid through the railway crossing barrier and into the train.

I took that brand new Ford LTD smack dab into the train. I don't know how fast the train was going, but it had to be at least 30 miles an hour and maybe a lot faster. My car eased in there at maybe two miles an hour and hit that onrushing train.

The fact that I am able to recount this story years later says something about the Lord. The Lord had a design and something for me to do. I should have been carried down that road, wherever it was, and been gone forever.

What happened was I woke up rather quickly. People have thought I made this up, but the honest truth is the first thing I saw was a big orange ball right in front of me. Why, I don't know. My car was raised up at about a 45 degree angle toward the train. All I could hear was "hippity-hop, hippity-hop, thump thump." I thought, "It's an alien."

I came to enough to know I had to get out of there, and I threw the car into reverse. Luckily it worked. I shot backward, like a stunt even Evil Knieval couldn't pull off. Why my car was up against the railroad cars like that and my car was just bouncing off them and not getting caught or dragging down the tracks I will never know.

I got out of the car and walked around the front. It was a total wreck. The front of the car looked like I had been in a butcher shop and somebody had sliced it all the way up. The engine was still running, but I don't know how. One headlight was working, but it was just hanging there.

The train stopped, and three guys came down and started ripping into me. I just stared at them. "Hold it right there," I said. "Wait a minute. We have a problem here. You guys are mad at me, but look at my car. My car is a total wreck. I think your train won. Nothing happened to your train, and you are ripping me. Screw you."

They said, "We're calling the cops." I said, "Call 'em."

The officer got there quickly. He talked to them, then he came over and talked to me. He took out his tape measure and went from my car to the train, then measured the skids and jotted it all down. He had gotten the conductor and the engineer calmed down.

I told them, "I didn't mean to run into your train. I was not attacking the train."

The officer finished making all of his notes, then he came over to me.

"From the distance involved and the skid marks, I estimate you were going 47 miles an hour when you hit the train," he said. I said, "what?" He repeated what he had just said.

"My dear friend," I said, "if I was driving 47 miles an hour when I hit the train, you and I would not be talking now. I tried to tell you earlier. I fell asleep, my foot came off the brake and I slid into the train. The skid marks you measured was when my rear end was roaring the other way, away from the train."

He looked at me and all of a sudden it hit him, and he started to laugh. He turned around to the conductor and engineer and told them to get back on the train and get out of there. Then he turned back to me and told me to take off.

I got back in the car and started to go, and then I realized—I was still lost. "The only thing I've found that I know is this train, and he's leaving." I told the officer, "do me a favor. I would love to get back to East St. Louis. Just get me to the river."

He did that, and finally I was on Interstate 55 headed toward my home near Fenton. Now it was about 4 a.m., and I knew there was a good chance I would get stopped by a Missouri Highway Patrolman and have to go over the entire story again. What happened to you? Well, first I had a train wreck. Luckily, nobody stopped me, and I made it home.

All I wanted to do was lie down and sleep, but as I walked into the bedroom, Mariana woke up, "Where have you been?" she yelled at me. I said, "I don't even want to talk about it." She insisted, but I was too tired. What had started off as a really fun night with a bunch of my buddies had just been a miserable experience for the past seven or eight hours.

I had been asleep about two hours when I felt a hand on my shoulder. It was my son Jimmy, who was five at the time. "Daddy, come downstairs for breakfast," he said. I knew what Mariana was up to. She was doing this on purpose. All husbands understand—she thought I was out having a good time and therefore she was going to punish me. I got up because it was my boy and went downstairs. I had to go to work anyway.

Mariana got up from the breakfast table and went outside and looked at the car. Then Kathy, our daughter, did the same thing. They both asked what happened, and the only thing I could think of, which I learned as either a player or a coach, was "no comment." I knew if I told them the truth, they would not believe it and think I had made up the story.

Then Jimmy did the same thing, and he's the only one I can talk to. "Shut up and eat your breakfast," I said.

I had to turn the car into McMahon Ford, and I had to repeat the story a couple of times. While I was telling the story, Mariana was sitting outside waiting for me, sweating in the heat and humidity, because our other car did not have air conditioning. Finally I came over and told her she could leave, that I was getting another car. She was none too pleased with me.

I really thought that was going to be the end of it, but I got a call from the insurance company and had to tell the agent the whole story. She couldn't help but laugh, too. I had managed to keep the whole thing from Bud until one day we were in a meeting, and Larry Wilson poked his head in about three times, saying little one-liners about the wreck.

Bud was looking at me, and after the third time I said, "Coach I've got to talk to you about something and I might as well do it now." I told the story again, and all of my good friends on the staff were doubled over because they were laughing so hard. Bud never even smiled. He had this real stoic look on his face, and I was thinking, "I don't blame him if he fires me."

He listened to the whole story and at the end he said, "Well I'll be damned," and he slammed his fist down on the table and broke into this gigantic belly laugh.

It turned out his twin brother had almost the exact same thing happen to him when he was a senior in high school in Minneapolis and he had escaped uninjured as well.

I looked at Bud and said, "God bless you. What a wonderful human being you are."

It wasn't over, however. The players naturally found out about it, and my good friend Tim Kearney went around calling me "choo choo" for weeks.

It was good we had some laughs, because when the season started nobody was laughing. It was a horrible year. We started off 0-8. I knew we were in trouble a month into the season when Bud came up to me and said, "I've got these guys together from Oklahoma. They want to buy the club."

He said, "We think we can buy the club. Do you think Bill will sell?"

I said, "No."

He wanted to know why not, and I told him the whole Bidwill family history in the NFL, but that didn't persuade Bud. He still tried to talk Billy into selling. He wanted to know who could get to him, who he would listen to. I told him Bob Hyland, who ran KMOX Radio. Bud and Hyland became close friends, and that ruined Bidwill's relationship with Hyland and started the end of Bud's tenure with the Cardinals even though he hung on into the next season.

Bud had his own ideas and programs that he wanted to implement, and they weren't always good ideas. One good thing about Bud was he would always listen to the opinions of other people, and he could be convinced to change his mind. We were in training camp at Lindenwood that year when he came up with an idea I knew was just awful, but I could not talk him out of it.

He said that while we were doing the two a days, the starting offensive linemen didn't need to be on the field for the first 40 minutes of practice. If we're starting at 2:30, tell them to be on the field at 3:15, Bud told me to go tell them that.

I told him, "Coach you can't do that." He was insistent.

I went to tell the guys, and of course they absolutely loved it. Going through the locker room they just sat there on the bench like five crows, all with big sarcastic grins. Have fun out there in the heat and humidity, they said. I was mad. It went against everything I believed in about the importance of team first, and to see their smirks drove me crazy.

I understood what Bud was trying to do. He knew those guys were older, he knew they could play and they didn't need that extra early stuff in practice. The rest of us were on the field when they came out and walked down the steps in the stands to get to the field. I was so ticked off it made me sick.

I went to Bud that night and said, "Coach, we can't do that again." He finally gave in. I went to the meeting room and said, "Well, that little party is over." They knew. The beauty of the whole thing was they totally concurred with me, they knew it was wrong. I didn't blame them. If I had been in their shoes, I would have done the exact same thing.

I think one of Bud's problems adjusting to the pro game was that he was so much smarter than everybody else.

He had a party at his house when we were something like 0-5. Mariana and I were the last guests to leave, and at the end of the party when it was just us sitting there, Bud said, "Well, what do you think, Jim?"

I looked around and made sure nobody else was there, and I said, "Coach, I know one thing you've got to do. I am so sick of your Saturday night speeches, I can't stand it." I told him about some of Coryell's speeches at the Saturday night team meetings, talking about what we needed to do to win, how we were going to do it and all that. I said, "That's what you've got to do. Get off the poems!"

Bud was a great speaker. As a public speaker there was no comparison between him and Coryell. But on Saturday night, talking to the players, that's a different deal.

I said, "Coach, you get up there, you start talking and you start to recite a poem. You're talking to them about Longfellow and Robert Frost. You've got guys sitting there, and maybe four or five of them have graduated from college, excluding the assistant coaches. They're thinking, 'Longfellow, Frost... isn't that the second-string right guard? No, I think he's the backup defensive end on the Jets or the Patriots'."

Bud looks at me and says, "You're kidding." And I said, "No, I'm not."

I said, "You've got to get down on their level to talk to them." I didn't mean to disparage him, but I thought it was something he needed to know.

I told the other assistant coaches before the next Saturday night that I had talked to Bud. I had him primed, and he was going to come into the meeting and deliver a real kick-butt speech. He had promised me.

I couldn't wait for that meeting. He stood up and said, "Gentlemen, here we are this evening, and this reminds me of Julius Caesar and the river Tiber." I kept waiting, and it doesn't happen. The other coaches looked at me like, what gives? I just shook my head. Obviously my message was forgotten.

It was a big credit to Bud, however, that he never changed during that losing streak. He kept the same attitude, kept working just as hard, and kept believing that it would turn around, and I'll be darned if that isn't what happened. We stopped that losing streak with a win at Philadelphia, and won three more in a row. We ended up winning six of the last eight games and wound up 6-10.

I had a tough decision to make at the end of that year, but I decided to leave St. Louis and go back to work for Don, who had taken over as coach of the Chargers. Our family had been so happy and comfortable in St. Louis and I really hated to leave, but I also missed working with Don. It also was a factor that it was San Diego, in southern California, but the biggest factor was being with Don again.

Before I left, Joe Sullivan called me into his office. He said. "We're offering you a lifetime contract." I said I didn't understand that, and he said, "The bottom line is for the rest of your life you will have a contract with the Cardinals." I said, "Joe I don't want it." I had never heard of that before in the NFL, and don't know if it had ever been done before. I had to make a quick decision. They thought they had me by making that offer, and I just said I was looking at the bigger picture and what I could do in life. I didn't always want to be an assistant coach for the Cardinals. And if I did want to do that, I told Joe, "You would be wrong for offering it to me." Those discussions ended pretty quickly.

Two secretaries, Nancy Keenoy and Geralynne Mason, organized a big surprise party for me. Tom Bettis and the other assistants kept me away, and when I walked in the room I couldn't believe it. Almost everybody in the organization was there, including a lot of players who had flown in from all over the country. It made me feel wonderful but at the same time made me realize I was leaving an awful lot of quality people.

That's one of the downsides of coaching, or playing, professional sports. Things can't stay the same. Conrad had been traded to New Orleans and was replaced by a good young player, Terry Stieve. Guys just can't stay together for very long.

By the same token, however, Don Coryell and I had a special relationship and always had so much fun together. Joe Gibbs came back from Tampa, Ernie Zampese came out of the scouting department to join the staff, Wayne Sevier was with us; it was a great staff. We also were going to create a pretty good team, one that actually should probably have won the AFC title and reached the Super Bowl that year. Tommy Prothro and the scouting department had done an excellent job of drafting some great players, including a rookie tight end from Missouri who went on to a Hall of Fame career, Kellen Winslow.

Just like in St. Louis, I got the chance to work with wonderful players, including Ed White and big Russ Washington. Both of those guys should be Hall of Fame candidates, but they don't have anybody pushing them other than me. Billy Shields played left tackle, the toughest position, and was the most underrated lineman on the team. He was very intelligent and tremendously coachable. He understood what I was teaching. He knew he could not be off three inches on his sets, or it would disrupt our plan. Even on a Friday afternoon after practice, Billy would ask me to stay after with him so he could check his sets. He knew if his first step was even a little bit off he was going to be in trouble.

We had two great wide receivers in Charlie Joiner and John Jefferson. Our quarterback was Dan Fouts. People are amazed when they ask me who the toughest players are that I've been around, and my answer is Conrad Dobler and Dan Fouts. Fouts?, they say, he's a quarterback. I say you're right, but I've never been around a tougher guy.

During one game, the guys were in the huddle and I flashed in a play. Fouts looked at me, then he started in on a player, and all of a sudden here the guy comes, head down, running to the sideline. I yelled for his backup to get in there, and when the guy got to the sideline I went over to him. "What happened, are you hurt?" I said. He shook his head no and said, "Danny kicked me off the field."

"He did what?" I said. He said, "He kicked me out of the huddle and off the field."

I turned away before I started laughing. I just went, "Wow, God bless Danny. This is beautiful." That's when you know the ship is right and you've got yourself a leader.

Fouts used to tell me, "Jim, if you see me holding onto the ball too long, you tell me."

I remember one time he dropped back, looked to his right and his primary area was covered. Then he turns to his left and checks deep, short, there is nothing there. In the meantime my guys are fighting like hell to keep the defensive guys away from our quarterback. It's been like six or seven seconds, and finally the defenders break through and hit Fouts just as he drops the ball off to a running back, who gets a couple of yards.

Danny got hit pretty hard, and his helmet was kind of knocked a little sideways, and he came by me as he ran off the field. I looked at him and I couldn't help myself. I said, "Hey Danny, I think you might have held the ball too long." He called me a couple of bad names, but I suspect he was smiling on the inside.

Fouts was one of those special players who stand out and deserve to be in the Hall of Fame. The thing that stood out about him more than anything else was his mental toughness. He knew he was going to get pounded, then he would simply get up and get ready for the next play. The game needs players like this.

The players coaches don't like are the false players. They can fool the fans and usually the media, but they can't fool the other players and the coaches. Those guys generally don't stick around too long.

In addition to working with Don and getting to know Fouts and the other great players in San Diego, I got a chance to meet Gene Klein, the team's owner. Usually the owner doesn't have much to do with assistant coaches, but Klein was an exception. The owner has to put up with the head coach, but he can ignore the assistants if he wants, and most do. Klein was a big bombastic man, and I enjoyed him.

He really helped me out when I got into a financial bind. I had not been able to sell our house in St. Louis, and we had a short-term loan to cover the down payment on the house we bought in San Diego. I was paying for a house in St. Louis, a house in San Diego and a short-term loan. That note was coming due, for $37,500, and because we still had not sold the St. Louis house, I didn't have the money to pay it.

I went to Klein and explained the situation to him. He blew up. He said, "Those no-good, mercenary rotten SOBs. Let me look into it."

The next day, I came in my office and there was a little white envelope on my desk. It just said Jim on the outside. Inside was a personal check from Klein to me for $37,500. That saved me, it absolutely saved me. Usually the offensive line has the longest meetings of any position. Not that day. They were dumbfounded, but I needed to get out of there to get to the bank.

We had a wonderful team, and I really thought was the best team in the AFC. It was the first time in Don's professional career that he also had a very good defensive team to go along with the Air Coryell offense. We played Houston in the playoffs, however, and lost. So much for going to the Super Bowl, and that really was a big disappointment.

About the middle of the season, the Cardinals finally decided hiring Wilkinson was a mistake and let him go. Larry Wilson took over on an interim basis, but when the season ended, they were looking for a new head coach.

A friend of mine in St. Louis called me and said, "Listen, I got this straight from the horse's mouth. What you've got to do is drop a note in the mail to Bidwill letting him know you are interested in the job." I said obviously Bill knew I was interested in the job, but my friend insisted. "This is what you need to do."

So I did. I wrote Bidwill a two-paragraph note, stating my desire to be a head coach in the NFL, and that I would like it to be with the Cardinals.

About a week went by, and one morning Don walked into my office. "I heard you wrote a letter to Bill Bidwill," he said. "What?" I said. "He just called me," Coryell said. "He said you had contacted him about the head coaching job."

I confirmed that was correct, and then Don said, "You don't want that job."

I looked at him and said, "Coach, it was good enough for you a few years ago." That stopped him. He had no reply.

Coryell's opinion was that I should bide my time and go after a job that had a better potential for success. My arguments were that there were only 28 head coaching jobs available (at that time) and how did I know I would get a better offer? I also liked St. Louis, knew most of the people there and could project what some of the problems would be.

I also was naive enough to think I would be able to solve them.

CHAPTER 6

My Turn

B ill Bidwill really tried to keep me from leaving St. Louis in the first place to rejoin Coryell in San Diego. In addition to the lifetime contract proposal, Bob Hyland, the head of KMOX, got involved and offered me a radio show if I would stay. I was not leaving with any bitterness, but I honestly felt I had severed my ties with Bill and the Cardinals.

My name had come up when there were openings for head coaching jobs in the NFL, and I really thought if I kept my nose clean I would have a shot at getting one of those jobs. I just didn't think it would be in St. Louis.

Even though I really did want the job, it still caught me a little off guard when Don walked into my office and said Bill had called to request permission to speak with me. I didn't hear from him until a week later. We were coaching at the Pro Bowl in Hawaii, and after the game I was back in my hotel room packing and getting ready to leave for the airport when Bill called. We agreed to meet two days later in San Diego.

The day that Bill arrived, it was pouring down rain. I agreed to meet him in a parking lot, because he wanted to be very secretive. I told him to follow me, and we would stop off and have lunch at a Mexican restaurant that was on the way to my house. It was managed by my friend Ray Ogas, who now works for the Rams.

I had not told Ray I was meeting with Bill, and when the two of us walked in for this secretive meeting, the first words out of Ray's mouth were, "Oh hi, Mr. Bidwill, how are you?" I thought, this was a mistake, but we sat down and had a good meal. Bill was all paranoid that the word was going to get out he was meeting with me, but I told him Ray wouldn't say a word, and he didn't.

It was still raining like a son of a gun, and I told Bill to follow me to my house. Mariana knew I was meeting with Bill, but she didn't know we would be coming back to the house. Because of the rain, our swimming pool was overflowing. We also had a creek right by our house, and the water had risen out of its banks. It was a flash flood in our backyard. Mariana was out there in this bright yellow slicker trying to keep the water away from the house. I didn't know if we were about to float away or not.

Bill started to talk about a contract, and told me what he was thinking, and I gave him my counter response regarding years and salary. We were in the kitchen, with all this commotion going on in the house. Mariana had come inside and her hair was soaking wet. Jimmy, who was three, was running around, we had cats and dogs and Jimmy had pet rats at the time; it was a real zoo. All of a sudden Bill stood up and said, "Well guess what, Jim?" and I said, "What?" and he said, "You're the new head coach of the St. Louis football Cardinals."

I looked at him and said, "You're kidding me?" He said no, I was the guy he wanted, and I said, "Well, God bless you. I will try my best to do as good a job as I can possibly do."

We came back to St. Louis the next day and Bill wanted to keep it secret. We were picked up away from the airport terminal by a van and whisked off to a hotel, where the team had called a news conference to make the announcement. It was an emotional time, and I won't apologize for being emotional. I definitely was crying tears of joy.

Even though I had only been gone a year, I found out a lot had changed with the team, mainly in attitude. Because the team had not been successful for a few years, the team was not playing with that confidence that had exuded from Don's teams. I knew we had to get that back if were going to be successful. We needed to make it a fun environment and put the fellows in positions where they had the greatest chances to succeed.

In one of my first news conferences, one of the reporters was all serious and asked questions about the pressure of being a head coach. I said, "Why don't you guys relax? There is no pressure about being the head coach. I've been facing pressure since I was 15 years old." The only difference in pressure between being an assistant coach and the head coach is having to answer to the owner. You also have to meet with the media, and they both want the same thing—answers—if things don't go the way you had planned. Why did you call this, why did you do that? I had enough confidence in myself to know that I could do that.

I had been back in St. Louis for about a week before I talked to Don in San Diego. He said, "You know who is really upset with you because you haven't called him? Gene Klein." Coryell was supposed to call him and tell him I was taking the St. Louis job before it was announced, but he never did. So I picked up the phone and called Gene.

"Who's this?" he said. "When I told him, he said, "Jim Hanifan, a no-good, rotten SOB."

I launched into my apology and explanation that I thought Coryell was going to call him, etc., and didn't do anything except continually say I'm sorry. In the back of my mind I'm also thinking about the loan, the $37,500. He finally said, "Jim, I think there's something else we need to talk about." I thought about stonewalling him but thought better of it! He might break on of my legs.

We ended the conversation by him telling me that he would always have a job for me if the situation didn't work out in St. Louis. I thought that was a great gesture, until he told me it would be shoveling manure for his horses.

I went back to looking at film of the Cardinals' previous season and tried to assess what had gone wrong on that team and where we needed improvement. I saw one thing that had not changed. Our kicker, Steve Little, was having problems as a rookie when I was here in 1978 and I saw it was continuing. Only a couple of weeks into the job I went to Bill and told him how messed up Little was with drugs.

Bill was shocked. I told him, "I told Bud (Wilkinson) about this two years ago." It turned out Bud had done nothing about it.

I told Bill, "I'm going to call him and tell him I know about everything that is going on, and if he continues to do that, he's gone." Bill asked me to meet first with Tom Guilfoil, the club's lawyer, and I did that.

Guilfoil didn't want me to say anything to Little about drugs. I didn't listen to him.

I called Little into my office and laid out the bottom line. "I know all about you, what's going on. I'll tell you another thing. If you think we are going to work our butts off around here and then you are going to miss a little chip-shot field goal because you are on cocaine, forget it. I'll kick the hell out of you. You will be out of here so fast you won't even know what hit you. You better think about it right now."

Little started crying, whether he was faking it or not, I don't know. I had my arm around his shoulders as he left the office. I told him to meet me and Chuck Banker, the special teams coach, at 10 a.m. the next day.

Ten o'clock came and went with no sign of Little. About 11:30 a.m., the receptionist got a call that he had been tied up because of car problems. I went into a rage. Around noon, he came sauntering down the hall.

I was on the phone when I saw him, and I just started yelling. I dragged him into the office and left the door open because I wanted everybody in the office to hear me. I wanted to grab his butt and throw him outside into the gutter, but I didn't do it. I said, "You are already on my s*** list. I am going to watch you like a hawk. You have already told me what kind of a guy you are. The first time I catch you, you're gone."

In the sixth game of the season, we were playing the Rams at Busch. After losing the first three games of the year, we had come back to beat the Eagles and New Orleans. A win over the Rams would get us back to .500 at 3-3.

We fell behind 14-0 in the first half, but Willard Harrell scored on a two-yard run, and then we scored a touchdown on a pass from Hart to Doug Marsh with about seven minutes to go. Little had already missed two 44-yard field goal attempts. But now all we had to do to be within a touchdown at 21-14, with plenty of time left, was for Little to kick the extra point. The kick was blocked.

I could see how deflated the team was. Chuck Banker came over and tried to say something about the snap being high, but I told him, "Charlie, don't worry about it. The guy's gone. It's a beautiful thing."

On Wednesday, three days after the game, we brought in another kicker, Neil O'Donoghue, to have a tryout against Little. If it had just been the two of them, plus Banker and me, on the field, I am sure Little would have won. But I kept the whole team on the field to watch and that psyched Little out. He lost, fair and square.

The next morning I cut him. I honestly did not feel bad about it because I thought he had done it to himself.

I got a phone call early the next morning telling me Little had been involved in a serious accident, hitting an exit sign on Interstate 270 during a heavy rainstorm about 2:30 in the morning. I knew people were going to say the accident was a result of him being released. I didn't feel that way then, and I still don't. He was just an accident waiting to happen.

The accident left Little paralyzed from the shoulders down. He died in 1999 at the age of 43.

Steve was not the only player who was involved with drugs. It was not a happy time, and coaches who have to spend their time worrying about problems like that instead of figuring out ways to win games know it makes your job a lot more difficult.

We had to move past that as a team, and I think we were able to do that. We had an exciting young running back in Ottis Anderson, but we were too inconsistent to have any prolonged periods of success. During my initial news conference, I had strongly proclaimed the one thing we wouldn't be was 5-11.

In the closing minutes of our final game against Washington, a 31-7 loss, I realized we were going to be 5-11. Don't think for a minute those reporters didn't constantly remind me of that. I would be sitting at home and on the 10 p.m. news, there I would be on the screen, predicting how we wouldn't be 5-11 again. I learned my lesson never to say things like that again.

Ottis was probably the biggest character we had on those teams. He knew from the first time he put on a uniform that he was above the rest of the team talent-wise, and that gave him a little more freedom than some of his teammates. Because we were such a young team, though, we really did not have anybody like the Dierdorfs and Doblers a decade earlier.

One incident I was reminded of years later came when we had just finished our meeting on Saturday night. The players were headed up to their rooms for bed, and as I walked through the lobby, I saw this young lady who looked kind of weird. There was something about her that didn't seem quite right. When I saw her duck and make a quick move up the stairs, I knew what was going on.

I got to the top of the stairs and opened the door into the hallway just in time to see a door closing, so I knew which room she was in. Otherwise, I wouldn't have known.

At an NFL Alumni dinner years later, one of the two players in that room decided to share this story with the audience.

"There was a knock on the door, and I yelled, 'Who's that?'" the player said. "'It's me, Coach Hanifan, open the door.' We rushed the young lady into the bathroom, closed the door and jumped into our beds. Coach stormed in and immediately accosted me because I was in the closest bed. He went on and on about how much he had done for me, how he had kept me because he thought I had such great character. 'Where is she? Where is she hiding?' He went immediately and pushed open the bathroom door and grabbed her and said go, and he didn't say it in nice words.

"My roommate was huddled up with his blanket over his ears trying to vanish into the night. Coach said he was going to think long and hard about what he was going to do to me. 'Have a nice evening,' and he left.

"I finally went to sleep, what could I do? We had a wakeup call for 7:30 a.m., and when I woke up about 7 a.m. I noticed my roommate was gone. He came back about 15 minutes later and when I asked where he had been, he said, 'To see Coach.' 'You did what?' I said. He said, 'I had to go tell him, it was me not you. Punish me, don't punish you.'

"He told him everything, and Coach said he appreciated the fact that he told him, and that he realized what was important. 'Maybe you learned a great lesson, and maybe your friend did, too.' He said only the three of us knew about this, and that's the way it was going to stay."

All I know is both of those individuals went out and had great games that day.

Despite all of the problems, I enjoyed being a head coach. I liked being in charge, being the leader. I enjoyed knowing all of the players and being with all of them, not just the offensive linemen. In truth, I found out being the head coach of an NFL team was not really all that different than being a head coach in high school. The biggest difference, of course, is the importance of the games and the fact that you are in a fishbowl.

Another similarity between the Cardinals and a high school team, that maybe wasn't the case with other NFL teams, was the number of players we were able to sign and bring to training camp. There were teams around the league that would bring in 150 players to training camp, but we could never do that. Those extra players allow you to give guys more rest during practice, and also you are often able to find some players who can help you, who for one reason or another slipped through the cracks and weren't drafted.

It was just the Cardinals' policy not to do that, and I could understand Bill's thinking. Bill didn't have the financial resources that a lot of other owners did, because the Cardinals were his only business. He couldn't tap into another business if he needed more money, and he didn't have other co-owners whom he could ask for more money. I knew that was going to be the situation, however, and you just have to make adjustments and deal with it.

I told the assistant coaches we were just going to run our practices like we were a high school team, and that's what we did. We still got guys hurt. On one occasion we were scheduled to scrimmage against the Chiefs in Charleston, Illinois, when I realized we couldn't do it. I would have to have played all of my starters, and risk further injuries, and I wasn't going to do it. John Mackovic was the coach of the Chiefs and I called him and told him the scrimmage was off. He got mad, but I didn't care.

Another difference between the Cardinals and many NFL teams is the influence that the coaches have on the draft. Again, that was a problem I was well aware of when I took the job, so I can't bitch about it. I knew from the years I spent with Don that a coach with the Cardinals would have no input on the draft.

That is the absolute truth. It was Bill's decision, and basically it boiled down to the fact that he wanted the scouting staff to be separate from the coaching staff. I can understand it to a degree. Bill was very loyal to his scouts, because he thought they were loyal to him. He didn't have the same feeling about his coaches, looking at them as mercenaries who would be moving on in a few years and he replaced by new coaches.

Our coaches were not allowed to go work out prospective players, and we didn't study films and grade guys like the coaches on other staffs did. Bill wanted it that way. I actually had to lobby him to let our assistant coaches go to the Senior Bowl. He asked me, "Why do you want them there?" I told him it was like a coaches' convention, and that they had worked hard all year and deserved to go. He made me promise him that they would not get involved with the scouts.

The head coach was allowed to be in the draft room, and I got to tell the scouting department what I thought our biggest needs were, but I didn't get to help select the players. The night before the draft, I literally would get down on my knees and say a rosary. "Lord somehow, some way, get us some good football players."

What happened was the scouts would love a player and select him, then the coaches would get him on the field and wouldn't like him. That would create a rift in the organization, and that happened all the time. In 1984 our scouts took Clyde (the Glide) Duncan from Tennessee. As soon as we got him on the field, all of our coaches were like, "How in the world did we draft this guy? He can't play."

We could have had Louis Lipps, who went to Pittsburgh and became the Rookie of the Year. Don't think we couldn't have used that guy.

Drafting players in any sport is not an exact science, and every team makes mistakes and picks guys who don't pan out. The problem with the Cardinals was that it happened way too many times.

When you combined the drafting problems with the roster limitations, we already were at a disadvantage from a lot of clubs. Two other factors working against us were that we could never get into the bidding for free agents coming down from Canada, and we were not allowed to stash players on injured reserve like a lot of teams.

Anytime the bidding on a player coming back from Canada got to be $25,000 or more, I knew we were not going to be involved. That was always a disappointment.

What made me more upset was the fact that even though a lot of teams would come up with phony injuries to, in effect, hide a guy on injured reserve for a year, we couldn't do that. You can't do that anymore, but teams got away with it back then.

If a team thought a guy was a good prospect but not quite ready to play, they would come up with a phony injury. That would allow the fellow to be paid for the year, work out all season and become a player who might be able to make the team and contribute the following year. Teams were kind of operating their own little farm teams that way.

When I brought it up, I was told we couldn't do that because it was illegal. I said I wasn't trying to turn other coaches in, but other teams were doing it, and all I wanted was a fair shake. Give me the same opportunities the other guys had, that's all I was asking. The answer was still no.

So all we could do was take the players we had and try to do the best we could with them. To be fair, not every draft pick was a bust. Ottis Anderson obviously was a great choice, and in 1981, we took linebacker E.J. Junior in the first round and quarterback Neil Lomax in the second.

In that draft, Lawrence Taylor and Hugh Green were both coming out and turned out to be awesome players. Both were gone when we picked, and we took Junior. I thought it was a good pick, and he started out like he was going to have a hell of a career. He also suffered from off-the-field problems, however, and didn't have the career he should have had.

When I first saw Lomax, I thought we were getting a hell of a quarterback. Jim Hart was still our starter and had enjoyed a great career. I don't think he has received nearly as much credit as he should for all of the great things he accomplished. He had been around a long time, however, and wasn't getting any younger. I knew we needed to find a young guy we could work with and develop to be ready when Jim was ready to hang it up.

The change came quicker than I expected. We were warming up before a game, and Jim threw about three long passes and he said, "OK, that's it." I said, "What do you mean, that's it?" He said he couldn't throw any more long ones in practice if he wanted to be able to throw the ball long during the game. I didn't like the sound of that.

I didn't want to be the person who took Jim Hart out of the starting lineup, but when I sat and looked at the overall situation, I knew the move had to be made. We had a lot of good young players, and I thought we might as well put in the young quarterback so they could grow up as a group. Believe me, it hurt me to do that. I had been with Jim a lot of years, and I didn't like it, but it had to be done.

I called Jim in the next morning and told him Lomax was going to be the starter. Jimmy was upset, and I didn't blame him, but I told him all the reasons. I also asked Jimmy to help Neil, because he was going to need help.

The press ripped me pretty good, but honestly I don't know what else I could have done. We could not have a tickertape parade downtown, and as much as I liked Jim and respected everything he had done in the game, the decision had to be made.

Lomax had a tremendous amount of ability. He had played in the run-and-shoot offense at Portland State and threw the ball about 60 times a game. He had really good field vision and a really good arm. I thought he had a chance to be outstanding.

One thing that worried me was his feet. He really had bad-looking feet. If you looked at his ankles you wondered how he could walk. He did have a lot of problems later in his life because of that and had hip replacement surgery at a very young age.

Neil went on to put up a lot of good numbers over the next few years, but never turned out to be the great quarterback I thought he could become. He had a good supporting cast in his receivers, Pat Tilley and Roy Green, and a great running back in Ottis Anderson, along with Stump Mitchell, but his offensive line and defensive team were average at best.

One of Neil's favorite receivers over the years was Roy Green, who came in as a defensive player. I was really ticked off at our wide receivers, other than Pat Tilley, and after practice one day I saw Roy running around, catching passes, and he was having so much fun. He had not played as well on defense as we would have liked, and as I watched him running around on the field, it hit me—let's move Roy to offense.

I went into the coach's meetings that night and told Emmitt Thomas, our receivers coach, to call Roy and tell him that he was being moved to wide receiver. Emmitt had a big smile on his face. Some of the other coaches said he couldn't do it, and one said Roy would never be able to do that. I said, "I didn't ask your opinion, he's doing it, and he's starting at wide receiver against the Redskins on Sunday."

I told our defensive coaches they could use Roy in nickel situations, but that was all.

Roy went out and caught five passes for 125 yards and a touchdown, and we beat Joe Gibbs and the Redskins. Near the end of the game, Roy came running off the field and said, "They're double covering me." I just looked at him and said, "Please. That will happen, but not yet."

Roy also intercepted a pass in the game while playing defense, becoming the first NFL player to score a touchdown on offense and intercept a pass on defense in the same game since 1957. That really was a move that made us a much more successful team.

I thought things definitely were moving in the right direction. We had improved to 7-9 in 1981, and actually made the expanded playoffs in the strike season of 1982. We went 5-4 in the regular season, then lost at Green Bay in the first round of the playoffs.

We were 8-7-1 in 1983, after losing the first three games of the season, and I knew we were knocking on the door of being a playoff-caliber team.

A couple of days after the 1981 season, Bill and I had a meeting to discuss the team. I was pleased with how things were developing, and thought Bill would be too. Out of the clear blue sky, Bill told me he was pleased with how the offense was working, but he thought we needed to make some major changes on defense. He told me to fire all of the defensive coaches.

I had a staff meeting scheduled for later that afternoon. I was literally stunned when Bill said that. I had to use some of my Irish blarney to get through the meeting without saying, "Yeah, I'm going to do that." Walking down the hall I thought, "Fire the defensive staff, yeah right, these guys have worked their butts off all year, and I'm going to fire them? That's not the Jim Hanifan I know. That will never happen around here."

About halfway down the hall I had made the decision, I wasn't doing it, so that wasn't the problem. The problem now was how would I circumvent the deal.

I walked into the meeting, and the coaches were all laughing and joking. We were getting ready to take a little break and have some time off, and I thought, "You guys wouldn't be very happy if you knew I was just told to fire you." We went through our meeting as scheduled, and when I got back to my office it was time to try to solve the problem.

After thinking about it a couple of days, I came up with the answer. I decided to create a new position, and put that coach in charge of the defense with a title of assistant head coach. I had to soothe some egos on the staff, but that was better than firing them. I liked what Detroit was doing defensively, so the guy I decided to hire was Floyd Peters, the Lions' line coach. Floyd and I had played ball together and been friends ever since.

The move worked, and Bill was pleased when the defense started jelling as well as the offense over the next couple of years.

We went into the 1984 season believing that we had enough talent to win—and we came about as close as a team could get. Going into the final game of the year, at Washington, all we needed to do was defeat the Redskins to win the Eastern Division title. The Redskins took a 23-7 halftime lead, but we battled back in the second half and went ahead 27-26 midway through the fourth quarter. Washington scored again, however, on a late drive which was helped by two penalties. E.J. Junior sacked Joe Theisman, and slam dunked him into the ground. Instead of it being fourth down, they got a first down and kept the drive alive. When Neil O'Donoghue missed a 50-yard field goal attempt as time expired, it was the Redskins who were the division champions and moved on the playoffs.

It took all of us some time to get over that loss. I knew we were that close to being a championship team, and I wondered if we would get that opportunity again. I was worried that we could never get over the hump. We had a lot of good young players, but not enough of them. It got back to the problems with the poor drafts, the lack of being able to get extra players into camp and not being able to keep guys on injured reserve. When we suffered injuries on top of that, we just had too many holes to fill, and we couldn't do it.

All of those problems came together in a disastrous 1985 season. I really think we could have made it without the injuries or the drugs, but we couldn't overcome that combination.

The injuries started in the first game. We beat Cleveland in overtime, but lost Roy Green to a high ankle sprain. He really was not 100 percent the rest of the season. We came home and pounded Cincinnati, when the Bengals were good but we also lost Lionel Washington, our best cover corner, and Thomas Howard, our best outside linebacker.

It was also about this point in the season when the drug problem really began to escalate. We had one player who we knew was on drugs, and who we also knew was not the smartest guy around. I called him into the office, and said, "Look, I'm not asking you to squeal on anybody or anything like that, but I need your help. I've got to find out how big this drug problem is on this team. When I call out a guy's name, you simply nod yes or no if he is on drugs, that's all I'm asking." He gave up everybody.

One of the guys we knew was on drugs. He had actually lived with his position coach the previous season. The player had been getting counseling and we really were trying to help him. By the third game of the season, in New York against the Giants, he was all messed up and didn't play. When we got back to St. Louis, I went in and told the team management, "Here's the deal. I'm cutting him. He's out of here, and here's the reason."

At that point in the season, I believe nearly one-third of our team, about 15 guys, were on drugs. I honestly believed that if we cut this one guy, it might send a message to the other guys that we were serious about cleaning up this problem and we could possibly keep those other guys in control. I also knew all of those guys were waiting to see how we handled this situation.

Bidwill didn't want to cut him. Even then he was thinking seriously about moving the Cardinals to another city, and our image around the country was that we were a good, young, exciting team. He was worried that if it got out that this team had a big drug problem, some of those cities that were interested in the Cardinals all of a sudden would not have been so interested. The young man stayed, and our drug problems got worse.

I thought about quitting, I honestly did, but I really didn't have the guts to do it. It would have been the smartest thing I could have done, to quit and call a news conference and say here's why I am quitting. I suspect I would have been a head coach somewhere else when the next season started.

It wasn't like our team was the only one that was ruined because of drugs. The problem was going on all over the league, and in major league baseball and the NBA, and really in society. But not taking any action against that one player really sent the wrong message, not only to our team but throughout the league. "They caught him and did nothing to him." Three or four weeks went by, he got caught again, and this time he went to a rehab center. By that time, the rest of the guys on our team didn't care.

The league was trying to deal with the problem. We had conferences and symposiums and listened to all of these so-called experts with their advice. I remember one psychiatrist came in to talk to a bunch of head coaches and somebody asked a question, "What is your success rate with your patients?" He said, "Well, I would like to say 50 percent, but to tell you the truth, it's not even 50 percent."

If this doctor is saying he can't cure even half of the people who come to him, what kind of success rate do you think we're going to have?

I can see why those players were drawn into drugs. It was so tempting and it was so hard to say no. Some players were strong enough not to succumb to that pressure. Others were from a small town or school, got drafted, were now in the limelight making a lot of money, and they were very vulnerable to the groupies who caused the problems. They had no idea how to handle their instant celebrity status, and many of them thought it was what they were supposed to do. By the time they knew better, they were hooked and there was no going back.

Despite all of that going on, we beat Green Bay after the loss to the Giants, improving our record to 3-1. Then the problems took over and we were in a free fall. We won only two more games the rest of the year and finished 5-11.

Our final game was on a Saturday against the Redskins. Bidwill had the locks changed at half time, but I didn't know that. We finished the game, I met with the team in the locker room and then I went in to the coaches locker room to shower and change. We had a function already scheduled for that evening for the players and their wives and the coaches and their wives in Clayton. My wife, Mariana, and the kids and another couple, good friends of ours, were waiting for me in the office upstairs.

I was showered and dressed when Bill came into locker room and sat down on a stool and said he needed to talk to me. "I'm going to let you go," he said. It took me by surprise.

It was a real emotional time. People don't think of Bill Bidwill being emotional, but he is. He was as broken up about it as I was. I was trying to comfort him. I was the one who had just gotten fired, and I was trying to comfort him.

It was very difficult going upstairs and telling the family. Jimmy was a freshman in high school at the time. As we started to walk out the doors of the stadium, he just broke down with these deep sobs. When that happened, that's what really ticked me off, seeing that he was hurting. My daughter, Kathy, also was highly agitated. As we got outside, we ran into Bo Bueckman, my good friend. He was talking about us getting together soon, and I just said, "Bo, look it's not a very good evening. I just got fired."

I went to the party in Clayton and broke the news to the team and my assistants. By that time the news had been announced, and all of the television cameras showed up. I didn't want to talk to anybody that night. Leonard Smith, our strong safety, went out into the lobby where all the TV folks were and said in a very intimidating way, "He doesn't want to talk to you. He will talk to you when he's ready. I want you out of here."

It would have been natural for me to blame Bidwill and still harbor a grudge against him, but I don't. I think Bill is a very misunderstood man by the media and the general public, and probably by a lot of people in football. He is a traditionalist. He is very proud of his father's franchise, and the role his father played in building the NFL. Charlie Bidwill was right there with George Halas, Art Rooney and Wellington Mara when it came to the history of the league. For that reason, Bill truly loves the NFL and has great respect for the league.

Bill has done a lot of great things for charities over the years, but he doesn't advertise it. He holds back on selling himself to the public and is very uncomfortable being in a public setting. He doesn't try to present himself to the public, and is not a social guy in group settings.

Whenever Bill is in a one-on-one situation, however, especially with someone that he knows well, he can be very social. He is witty and very caring. He has been very loyal to a lot of people in his organization.

People would try to belittle him over the years, and he would try to play it like it didn't bother him, but nobody likes that. He would not react and never come out and tell somebody to stick it. He is a very complex human being.

One of Bill's faults, I think, when it came to his football operation was the trust that he put in the scouting department. It still frustrates me to think how close we were to being a championship club, and how we had to do it with all of the poor drafts and other problems stacked against us.

After I had been gone from St. Louis for several years, Joe Sullivan and his wife, Joanie, visited us at our cabin at Lake Tahoe. Joe was as close to Bill as anybody, working as his general manager for a long time. As we sat there and talked about the old times, Joe told me, "I don't know if you ever knew this. I went and talked to Billy and told him how great I thought everything was going, how we had the right coach and everything was just getting better and better. But there is one thing we've got to change—the scouting department."

Joe told me that Bill wouldn't hear it. Even though Joe was prepared and knew he would have to argue hard, Bill cut him off. "I'm telling you, I told him," Joe told me. "He was adamant that was not going to happen."

I am not going to knock Bill Bidwill. He owned the team and therefore he called the shots. A coach has to do what he can within the parameters he is given. That's all you can do.

A couple of things I am proud of about my tenure as a head coach is that I had people tell me I never changed as a head coach. I have seen assistants who did change as a head coach, becoming less friendly to their players and acting more important. I'm glad that didn't happen to me. I'm glad I was just as good of friends with all of the players as I had been with my offensive linemen over the years.

Last year when the Rams were in Seattle, the value of relationships between a coach and his players was driven home to me. I went to dinner with Stafford Mays, a defensive end on the Cardinals when I was the head coach, and his family. Big Ed Simmons, who had played for me with the Redskins, drove up from Spokane; Dale Nosworthy, who I had recruited out of high school to Utah and played there for me, drove over from Idaho; and one of my high school players, Hal Teel, who lived in Seattle. The only common link between these fellows was me, and as we sat there and talked, these guys from different walks of life and different levels of football, I could see a bonding taking place.

It was really special to see. I don't know if all of those guys saw it happening and thought about it, but I did.

One thing that bothers me about the coaching profession is when a coach gets so entranced with himself that he thinks he is the game. I've seen it happen with coaches, and I've also seen it happen with players. Some players think they are the game. I've got news for all those folks—they aren't the game. The game is the game.

One time while I was the head coach I was asked to be a judge at a beauty contest. Why, I don't know. One of the other judges was one of the local television weathermen. As the evening wore on, he was up there signing autographs and acting like a big celebrity. He was the weatherman. I couldn't believe it.

I think the same thing about coaches. The media makes them out to be celebrities, and a lot of them get caught up in the talk and begin acting like they are celebrities. I can't understand that.

I was proud of the relationships I developed with the media. I've seen head coaches, and assistants for that matter, who don't want anything to do with reporters and view them totally as the enemy. I never did that.

I was fortunate that during five of my six years as the head coach, I had the same two guys as the beat writers for the St. Louis newspapers, John Sonderegger for the *Post-Dispatch* and Dennis Dillon for the *Globe-Democrat*. They were both good, fun guys and good reporters, and they were both quality professionals.

It was as if both of them were part of the team, because they were there every day, just like the players, from the start of training camp to the final day of the season. They were human when they wrote their stories and most important, they were fair and objective. They weren't out to just rip somebody for the heck of it, and that is sometimes the case.

Sometimes they were tough, and they had a right to be. One Monday after we had played a really poor game the day before, I could tell the players were mad and ticked off about the stories in the newspapers. I told the team, "I'm glad that's the way you feel. But it's amazing to me that you are ticked off at the writers. What do you think they should have written about your exploits on the gridiron? What kind of endearing terms should they have bestowed on you? Get off it. You played like s***. They were writing what they saw. I don't blame them one bit. I'd do the same thing and in reality, if you were the writer you would do the same thing.

"Let me explain one thing to you. If you want people to write good things about you, or say good things about you, then get off your butts and play that way. That is the bottom line."

During my speech, I could see some of the players' emotions changing, going from being defiant to ashamed of their own thoughts. They knew I was right.

On days after a bad weekend, Dennis and John didn't want to look at me when they came walking into the office. I'd look at them and basically say the same thing I said to the players. "I don't blame you guys."

There were times we had disagreements, when I didn't think a story was accurate or I thought they had overstepped their boundaries. I would talk to them and we would work it out. Five minutes later I would have my arms around them.

Because I had that relationship with Dennis and John, I didn't have the problems a lot of coaches have with the media. You see it, especially among younger guys, when they come into a job and are trying to create a name for themselves and stroke their own ego. It usually doesn't take long for them to get knocked down a couple of notches.

There was one young writer who began covering the team in 1985, and he wrote a lot of negative articles about me and the team. I don't know if they were a factor in my getting fired, but it sure didn't help.

Owners in professional sports are like athletic directors in college. The AD's always have certain alums that they are beholden to because they are big financial boosters of the school. If somebody writes a story in the paper and the alum happens to agree with the writer and says something to his good buddy the AD, well the AD is going to listen a lot to his buddy because of his financial support. But his buddy might never have said anything if he hadn't read the story in the newspaper.

The owner of a pro team is the same way. He has his rich friends, and they read the paper, and they have their opinions about whether they agree with a writer or not. They will most likely say to the owner, "I read that story in the paper, and I agree (or disagree) with it. You need to be thinking about getting a new coach." The owner will listen to his friend more than the writer, but the idea was planted in his friend's head by the writer.

A classic example of this is Tom Guilfoil, a friend of Bill Bidwill and a well-connected and powerful attorney in St. Louis. He became the confidant of Bidwill after Bidwill's relationship with Bob Hyland came to an end. He had a pretty sweet deal when you think about it—he didn't have any money tied up in the team, he didn't really have any responsibilities and he was getting paid what I am sure was a pretty comfortable sum to offer his suggestions.

This man never played one snap of football in his life, he never coached one day of football in his life. Yet here he was telling the owner who should stay and who should go.

Guilfoil has a lot of scalps on his belt, and one of them is mine.

I remember the first time I met the man. He had the big desk with the chair, sitting up high, like a throne. The visitor's chairs were small, like you were a little child, and he was going to talk down to you. I went in his office to talk about the Steve Little situation.

The way he talked was that he leaned forward and spoke almost in a whisper, so you had to lean forward and strain to try to hear what he was saying. I didn't do that. I leaned back instead and I responded to him in a very soft voice. When he mumbled, I mumbled, and I got him going, "Huh, what?"

When I left his office and walked back to the stadium and the team's offices, I ran into one of our young lawyers, Bob Wallace, and he asked if I had met Mr. Guilfoil. I said, "Oh, you mean mumbles?" From that time on, Guilfoil never knew that was his nickname.

Guilfoil's other scalps include Gene Stallings, Buddy Ryan and Joe Bugel, he got us all. He probably is still getting guys. He really doesn't like anybody. The only person he likes is Tom Guilfoil. He ought to coach the Cardinals—that's the answer.

The morning after I was fired, my phone rang about 8 a.m. When I answered it, it was my good friend Whitey Herzog, the manager of the baseball Cardinals. Whitey started talking and I was going "Yeah, right, uh-huh." Whitey stopped talking and then he said, "You're not listening to me, this is going in one ear and out the other." He was correct, so I started paying more attention.

"I know exactly how you feel, because the first time I got fired I felt exactly the same way," Whitey said. "The second time …. And the third time …"

I interrupted him. "You got fired three times?" Suddenly I didn't feel so bad. "Each time I wound up with better jobs after I got fired," Whitey said. His call really picked me up and I never forgot it.

In the next few days I received calls from almost all of the head coaches in the NFL. Joe Gibbs called and said, "I know everything that has gone down over there and what you had to go through." Bill Walsh called me the night before the 49ers were playing a playoff game. A lot of other people, from the equipment people to the trainers and secretaries called too, and that really lifted my spirits.

I still had a year to go on my contract, and a lot of my fellow coaches advised me to take the 1986 season off, relax and recharge my batteries ready to come back strong the following year. That sounded like a good idea to me.

CHAPTER 7

Wearing
Enemy Colors

For the first time in my life, I wasn't playing or coaching football. I still wanted to remain involved with the game, however, because I honestly expected to be back coaching somewhere the following year.

A friend of mine, Mike Giddings, had started a company called ProScout Inc., so I went to work for him. I wasn't getting paid, because I was still under contract to the Cardinals, but I scouted games every week in Kansas City, Indianapolis, Chicago or Cincinnati. They were all easy drives from St. Louis, and I got to see a lot of my friends and maintain my contacts and connection with the game.

Only three or four jobs opened up the following year, and Marion Campbell got the job as the head coach in Atlanta. Rod Dowhower was fired in Indianapolis, and we agreed that we would like to go someplace together. Campbell wanted both of us, so we packed up and moved to Atlanta.

We had a good group of offensive linemen, including Mike Kenn, who was an outstanding tackle. He made some All-Pro teams despite the team not being very good, and that is tough to do. We didn't have a big-time quarterback or running back or wide receivers, so we had a difficult time moving the football. We had some scrappy players on defense, but our offensive problems really kept us from becoming a competitive team.

We had some other problems, including drugs. In our third year there, a really good young promising tackle, Ralph Norwood, who had been a second-round draft pick, was killed in an automobile accident. There was no evidence of drugs or alcohol. It was just an accident. He was a great kid and it was a terrible blow to the team, coaching staff and organization.

Marion finally got frustrated with all of the problems, and he resigned with four games left to go in the year. The management came to me and asked if I would be the interim head coach. You talk about a tough job, but I said OK.

Before our first game, somebody came out in the newspaper and said nobody on the current staff would be considered for the head coaching position. That wasn't a shock to me. Coaches never get hired off losing staffs, and the biggest thing the Falcons needed was to sell tickets. A couple of the coaches were ticked off, but I didn't blame the Falcons a bit.

I addressed the team plus the coaching staff. I said, "Let me explain something to you. All of the coaches are going to be out of here after the season. Wake up to reality. But we're going to be coaching somewhere next year. Here's the main point—all of the other people in the NFL are going to be looking at you fellows the next four games to see how you perform. It's easy to go down. It behooves you to play out of your rear ends and for us to coach like sons of guns. We are all in the same boat."

Our first game was against the 49ers, and that was when they really had it going with Joe Montana and Jerry Rice and everybody else. Before the game, I get a message that Rankin Smith, the owner of the Falcons, wanted to see me. I had not talked with him when I took the job, everything was done through his son Taylor, who really was running the club on a day-to-day basis.

He said, "Jim, I just want to thank you for being the head coach. I appreciate your efforts and I want you to know what the newspaper said about nobody being considered for the head coaching job is a bunch of hogwash. You definitely will be considered."

I looked at him and said, "Mr. Smith, there is no way in hell you can possibly consider me for crying out loud. You've got to get somebody in here who's been winning, you can't have one of us."

He said, "Well Jim, let me ask you this. What about if you win the next four games?"

I said, "Mr. Smith, if we win the next four games, you should definitely hire me because I will be a miracle man. If we win two out of the next four you ought to hire me because we will have done wonders."

We played the 49ers tough but screwed it up in the second half and lost. The next week we had the Vikings at Minnesota. We had a couple more goof ups in that game and lost, too. Next we played the Redskins, and we were ahead 24-10 at the half. The Redskins scored with just about a minute to go in the game to go ahead.

Deion Sanders was a rookie that year, and he was an amazing athlete. He had already broken a long punt return in the game, but his shoulder was hurting so we had taken him off special teams. Standing on the sideline, I hear this, "Coach, coach, coach," so I turn around. It was Deion.

"Put me back in there and I can run that SOB back," Deion said. I told him, "Thanks for offering, but I don't want to risk hurting your shoulder." He kept insisting that he could do it. There literally were sparks coming out of the kid's eyes.

Finally I said, "OK, get in there."

The Redskins kicked off, and the ball went right to Deion. He got some blocks, although he was the kind of player who really didn't have to have many blocks to get open. He could make all of the cutbacks and reads so well he created all of his own holes.

I'll be darned if he didn't go flying up the sideline, right past the Redskins' bench. He got to about midfield, and the only Redskin left was the kicker, Chip Lohmiller. He dove just as Deion was cutting back to his left. I really thought Deion was going to score and we were going to win the game.

As Chip dove, however, by luck his hand hit Deion's foot and knocked him off balance. He fell, or otherwise he would have scored and we would have won the game. Joe was coaching the Redskins and he told me later as Deion was running up the sideline, his heart was in his throat. Deion really was a great player.

We lost the final game as well, to Detroit, but I never will forget one of our players, Rick Bryan, a defensive tackle, who came up to me after the game. He said, "Coach, I've had more fun these last four weeks than I've had in a long time. You brought the fun back in the game."

That was one of the nicest compliments I could receive. Football is a business, and you have to be serious and dedicated to be successful. But you also have to be able to have fun, or you are going to view it strictly as a job, and you are going to get awfully tired of putting in all of those long hours rather quickly.

Each coach and player started playing the game when they were young for one reason—it was fun. Too many people forget that when they get into pro football.

One of the more memorable football experiences of my life came that year, when I got to go to Michigan State for Tony Mandarich's workout prior to the draft. It was awesome. It was the greatest workout for an offensive lineman in the history of the game.

He did everything you could ask a guy to do. He did the vertical jump, the bench press, the 40-yard dash, he was unbelievable. If there ever was a player coming out of college who I thought was headed for stardom in the NFL I thought it was Mandarich.

What happened to him shows you how uncertain this business is, for coaches and players. Two other great players were in the draft that year, Troy Aikman and Barry Sanders. Dallas had the first pick and took Aikman. Green Bay was second, and the Packers selected Mandarich. I thought it was a great pick. Detroit picked third and took Sanders.

What would have happened to Lindy Infante, the coach of the Packers, and to the NFL if Green Bay had chosen Sanders instead of Mandarich? Barry Sanders and Brett Favre on the same team, are you kidding me, mother of God. It would have been like Kurt Warner and Marshall Faulk. Mandarich turned out to have all kinds of problems, I guess caused by steroids, and never panned out. Infante got fired two years later. If they had picked Sanders, Infante might well be in the Hall of Fame today.

If any coach or scout says they never made a mistake on a player, they're lying. It happens, and there isn't anything you can do to prevent it, except hope you get lucky.

With the season over, I wasn't certain what I was going to do next. There were some head coaching positions open, but I didn't know if I would be considered for any of them. Joe Bugel was the offensive line coach with the Redskins, and he was involved in the interviewing process with the Falcons. I had recommended him, along with my buddy from San Diego, Ernie Zampese.

It turned out Bugel was hired as the new coach of the Cardinals, who had moved to Phoenix. That left his old job as offensive line coach with the Redskins open. Gibbs called and wanted me to fly up to Washington.

Joe picked me up at the airport and we went to dinner. We had breakfast the next morning, and all we needed to finalize the deal was for me to meet the owner, Jack Kent Cooke. Joe drove us to Redskins Park, and as he pulled into his reserved spot, I looked at the wall of the building and it was this giant Indian head logo. It was the Redskins' logo and it was probably 50 feet or so high. I looked at the logo and thought about all of the years I had hated the Redskins.

I told Joe, "I can't do it. It's over." I was really serious. Joe looked at me and started laughing. He said, "What are you talking about?"

I said, "I've hated the Redskins for 15 years. I can't turn that off."

Joe said he had gone through the same thing when he got hired as the head coach, but assured me I would get over it quickly. We went into the offices and he called to set up the meeting with Cooke.

Cooke lived on a magnificent estate in the Virginia countryside. Before we got there, Joe told me, "Don't be humble. The guy does not like humble people."

Cooke was a short man, maybe 5-foot-6 or so, but he had his desk elevated and these little chairs for visitors in front of him so it looked as if he were towering over them. We shook hands and sat down and Cooke blurted out, "Well, what are you going to bring to the table?"

I was so intimidated I forgot Joe's advice. "I hope to …" I started to say before he interrupted.

"You hope to?" Cooke yelled. "I don't need any hope. I just lost one of the best coaches I've ever had. And what the hell are you going to do?"

I lost it. He made my Irish dander rise, and I didn't care what happened.

"Forget I said that," I said back to him. "I'll tell you what I'm going to do. I'll do twice the job that anybody else can do. That's what I'm going to do. You'll find out about it."

That took him back a little bit, because even if he didn't like people to be humble, I don't suspect this powerful, wealthy man was used to his assistant coaches barking at him the way he barked at them. I think Joe laughed all the way back to the office.

Everybody who worked for the Redskins was nervous around Cooke, because he would just walk in one day and fire somebody. The public relations folks were nervous wrecks, because they would have to be on the lookout for him all the time. He never bothered the coaching staff, but he did like to come to practice, and he liked entertaining all of his rich and powerful friends.

One day Cooke could bring out members of his family, other times it would be a senator or the governor. He expected the head coach to come over and talk to him before practice, and a couple of times I was filling in running the practice, so I had to do that.

Cooke wanted to know my opinion about a couple of players, and I was being real guarded, because I didn't want to say the wrong thing. He said, "I asked you and I want to know what you think, right now," so I had to tell him.

One time Cooke was kidding around and asked me, "How old are you?" I think I was 63 at the time and told him that. He puffed out his little chest and said, "I'm 81."

I don't know why, but I was in a mood to kid around with him. I said, "Is that right? You don't look a day over 63."

Then I continued and probably went a bit too far, but luckily Cooke didn't blow up and fire me on the spot.

"You know Mr. Cooke, when I go on the road, I've got to tell you, some people think I'm you." He said, "Is that so?"

Then I said, "You know, the more I think about it, there might be something to that. I might be your illegitimate son."

As soon as I said it, I cringed. Why did I say that? Cooke was silent. I thought, "He isn't going to take this for a joke," and then he let out this big guffaw. I was able to breathe again.

Cooke loved Joe, and he should have, because Joe brought him three Super Bowl championships. I wasn't there for the first two, but I got to experience that feeling in 1991.

We had a good team my first year in Washington, going 10-6, making the playoffs. We lost a couple of tough games, then beat the Eagles in the playoffs before losing to San Francisco.

Joe had been right about how quickly I would forget about my hatred for the Redskins. It really only took a few days, walking around the office and meeting people, to realize what a great place it was. One wonderful woman, Barbara Frye, worked for all of the coaches, and she was and is a very special lady.

I had only been with the Redskins a few weeks when I called Dierdorf on the phone. "You won't believe what is going on here," I told him, "it's déjà vu. It's like I've gone back 20 years in a time machine. These guys are just like you guys were. There's a guy like you, and a guy like Conrad and a guy like Tommie." It truly was amazing.

The player most like Conrad, vocally and by being a great player, was Russ Grimm. He is coaching with the Steelers now and really should be in the Hall of Fame. He always had the quips and was just so funny, so I guess in reality he was kind of a combination of Dobler and Dierdorf. It was amazing, because the questions were the same and the expressions were the same. I never thought it would happen to me again in my lifetime.

Jeff Bostic was like Banks, he was undersized but very productive. Joe Jacoby was a great player, and he and Grimm were really the two who helped launch the term "The Hogs" for the offensive linemen. Jim Lachey was there as well, and he was a great player.

One of the things those offensive linemen did was start their own club. They called it the 5 o'clock club, because every Thursday after practice was over around 5 p.m., they would get together in a shed near the practice fields and sit there and relax and drink beer, They always had somebody get the beer and ice it down so it was good and cold and they could come right over after practice and start drinking.

It was a very big honor to be included in the club. There were a lot of great players on the Redskins, including Pro Bowlers and Hall of Famers, who were never admitted into the club. They brought John Riggins in, even though he was a running back, because he was one of them. He probably was the biggest single character on the club.

Donnie Warren, the tight end, was in the club, and so was Terry Orr, the H back. It had a lot to do with what kind of individual you were. You had to measure up to what those linemen wanted someone in "their" club to be like.

Donnie grew up across the street from my brother in Los Angeles and went to my old high school. When Kathy was a little girl, they actually got in the wading pool together during the summer.

I was invited to the club one time because they were initiating a new member, Mark Schlereth, who had just received his first All-Pro and Pro Bowl selections. They had a big party for him, and I enjoyed myself tremendously.

The funniest thing about the club was that Gibbs knew about it, but he actually thought it had been disbanded. These guys were still meeting at that shed every Thursday at 5 p.m., and Joe said to me one time, "Well I'm sure glad those guys don't do that anymore." I almost fell over.

There wasn't much that got past Joe, however, and I think he knew based on the team's success in 1990 that we were going to have a chance for a good season in 1991. We had basically the same team coming back, and it turned out Joe was right.

When Joe's first team had gone to the Super Bowl and come up with a great game plan, he was determined it was because the coaches had worked so hard—averaging working until about 4:30 in the morning each Monday, Tuesday and Wednesday night. Joe and I had always worked long hours in St. Louis and San Diego, sleeping on very uncomfortable tables in the training room a couple of nights a week.

It was kind of frustrating to watch the defensive coaches going home by 10 p.m. at the latest, so I guess my advice to young coaches is to stick with defense. You will get a lot more sleep.

Nobody wanted to look at their watches when we were in those all-night meetings, and you really didn't want to know what time it was. We learned very quickly, however, that the garbage man came at 3:30 a.m., so we knew when we heard the dumpster that was what time it was. The next signal was the Concorde flying over on its way to landing at Dulles Airport. That was 4:30 a.m. "Guys I just heard the plane go over," somebody would say.

We actually had a thesaurus in the room to try to come up with names for all of the shifts and motions on the plays. We actually argued about what to call the plays.

After one of our very late night sessions, one of the coaches said he was going to sleep on a mattress and sleeping bag on his office floor. He asked me to wake him up when I got back to the office. We had a meeting at 8:45, and I got there about 8:15, so I decided to complete some paperwork and let him sleep a few extra minutes.

The restrooms at Redskins Park were on the opposite end of the building from the coaches' offices. I was sitting at my desk when his door opened and he walked out in his shorts, carrying this ziplock bag. He didn't know anybody was watching him. He walked down to the fire escape, opened the door, and emptied the bag outside. When he got back I said, "Hey, that's quite an idea." It was one of the funniest things I have ever seen.

Coaches, and most players, are creatures of habit. I was walking home from the library one time in college when I was having a really good year and I came across a black cat. I must have walked a mile out of my way so I didn't have to cross paths with that cat. Joe was convinced the reason the Redskins had a good game plan and won that Super Bowl was because the coaches worked so late, so that was what we had to do.

It did make for some tired coaches, and for some humorous incidents. One thing all coaches who are so tired are afraid of is falling asleep in front of the players while watching film. It happened one time to a Rams coach in the 1950s, and all of the players snuck out and left while the coach was snoozing. I was always afraid of that happening to me.

The whirring of that projector would take you right into dream land. We were watching film one day and I tried to point out a mistake made by Ed Simmons, our right tackle. I showed him what was wrong with his technique and his footwork, and then I dozed off. My reflexes were still working, however, and I was running the film back and forth with my hand but I didn't know it. When I came to, we were still watching the same play, but I thought we were later in the game. I tore into Ed again. "How many times do I have to tell you?" Joe Jacoby spoke up. "Jim, you already talked to Ed about that. You were sleeping, weren't you?" They couldn't keep themselves from laughing hysterically.

That wasn't as bad as what happened one time while we were in San Diego. Joe, Ernie and I were watching film after we lost 28-26 to Atlanta on a last-minute play. We were 10-3 at that point and having a great year. Gene Klein, the owner, came in the film room but we didn't see him or hear him. He flipped on the light and turned off the projector. "And they told me I had the best coaching staff in the NFL. S***." Then he turned and walked out. Joe's face was beat red. We were all ticked off.

We were playing at New Orleans the next week and I was out on the field early, checking to make sure all of the phones to the press box and everything was working OK. I looked up, and Gene was walking toward me. He had on a Chargers shirt, with the big lightning bolt, and he looked to me like Captain Marvel. He came up to me and said, "Well I hope we've got everything straightened out this week."

I had a pretty good relationship with him, especially for an assistant coach. I said, "Well, here's what we are going to do. We're going to try to keep it close, and then pull it out at the end. We're in the entertainment business, you know."

It was my way of getting back at him for the shot he had given us, but I was suddenly worried I had gone too far. He turned around and stormed off. Thank the good Lord we had such a good team. We won 35-0, and he didn't say a word to me about it.

The Redskins in 1991 also were an outstanding team. We started the year 11-0 before losing to Dallas. We won the next three games, and had everything clinched—the division title, the first-round bye and home-field advantage throughout the playoffs—going into the final game at Philadelphia.

Our offensive line was in position to break the record for fewest quarterback sacks allowed in a season, six. When we got ahead 17-7 in the third quarter, we started pulling all of the starters out because we didn't want to get anybody hurt. The Eagles sacked us three times, wiping out our chance at the record. That has to be one of the greatest offensive lines in history! Jacoby and Lachey at tackles, Bostic at center and McKenzie, Schlerieth and Grimm at guards.

Joe came up to me on the sideline near the end of the game and said how sorry he was we didn't get the record. I told him not to worry about it, but now we really had to go on and get that Super Bowl.

We did not allow another sack in the two playoff games and the Super Bowl. Nine sacks in 19 games—I think that has to be some kind of record, and I know it is a remarkable achievement.

We beat Atlanta and Detroit in the playoffs to win the NFC Championship and earn the right to play Buffalo in the Super Bowl in Minneapolis.

I had been to Super Bowls before as a spectator, but that is an entirely different situation. You are having a good time, relaxing with your buddies, and you really don't have an emotional attachment to what happens in the game.

Being in the Super Bowl was an awesome experience. I was in awe. We had the extra week between the conference championship games and the Super Bowl that year, so all of our work was done the week before we even went to Minneapolis. When we got there, basically everything was done. All we had to do in the evening was watch the practice film, review our notes for the next day and we were done. We were able to complete our work by 10 p.m. and go out and enjoy ourselves with our family and friends.

As we were getting ready to head onto the field for the game, I told some of the players in the tunnel, "It's just another game fellows, just another game." The guys jerked their heads around, and you could tell by the look in their eyes they knew that wasn't the case at all.

Luckily we played well and won, 37-24. With a couple of minutes to go in the game, I knew we were going to win, and I honestly thought of all of the people I had spent so much time with during my coaching career. I thought about Don Coryell, and Dierdorf and Dobler and Banks and the rest of those players. I remember saying to myself, "I really wish you guys were with me right now, so you could experience this." I know it may sound phony, but it's the truth. They all had been so instrumental in getting me to that point.

Joe came over and gave me a big hug. "I'm so happy you got yourself one," he said, meaning the ring.

Joe is a special person and a great friend. Our relationship began when we were together on Coryell's staff in St. Louis, and we have maintained that friendship for more than 30 years. He knew I had been a head coach for six years, but I knew he was running the show and it was never an awkward situation for either of us.

A lot of head coaches will never hire a former head coach for an assistant's job on his staff because he is afraid of them. That coach knows that if one of his assistants has head coaching experience, the owner might look to fire him and move that guy in at the first sign of trouble. It was a tribute to Joe that he never worried about that.

We would argue about strategy or something, but then I would come back a few minutes later or the next morning and say, "You know I was thinking about that, and I think you were right." Then Joe would say, "I was thinking about it too, and I decided you were right." Then we would argue again, from the opposite viewpoint.

Joe was just as competitive as I was, and when we were on Don's staff, we both wanted to be head coaches. By the time I joined his staff in Washington, I had spent six years as a head coach, and he had already been the head coach of the Redskins for nine years. A lot of the way he coached came from Coryell, but he also was a composite of all of the coaches he worked for. He created a real fun environment and working atmosphere for the coaches, and I think it is a great tribute to Joe that none of his assistants ever left his staff because they were fired or quit because they were unhappy. The only way people left was to become a head coach somewhere.

One of the most enjoyable nights of my life came when we went to the White House after winning the Super Bowl. Some of the players who had been there before warned me not to get excited; they said we would go in, take a few pictures, and be back on the bus in an hour and a half maximum.

Well we got there about 4 p.m., and stayed until 10 p.m. The White House staff set up a big tent on the lawn and served a great Mexican dinner. Everybody got their pictures taken with George and Barbara Bush, and they could not have been nicer or more accommodating.

During the evening it started to rain, and everybody tried to crowd under the tent, but we could not all fit. I will never forget the sight of Barbara Bush, the first lady, standing at the door in a flowery print dress with one red tennis shoe and one blue tennis shoe. She was trying to shoo people into the house—the White House—to get out of the rain. People were scared and reluctant, but she kept insisting. "Come on, come on, get in the house," she said. We had mud and grass on our shoes, but Mrs. Bush didn't care. As Mariana said later, it wasn't like she was going to have to clean the place up by herself.

President Bush had some games set up, including a basketball hoop, but his favorite game is horseshoes. He is a very good player, plus he had a ringer, somebody off his staff. They made it into the finals and won.

I happened to be standing only a few feet away from the President about 7 p.m., when one of his aides came up to him and said, "Sir, we are going to close this down in about 15 minutes." The President's response was, "Chill out, I'm having fun, let it go."

It was an awesome evening, and one that probably will never be duplicated, because the Redskins were Washington's team and this was their third Super Bowl victory. Both the President and Mrs. Bush were just terrific, and it was really like they were your next door neighbors, that's how they made you feel about them.

Most of the same team was together in 1992, and we had a good season. We again made the playoffs but injuries devastated us and we couldn't get back to the Super Bowl. The biggest loss came after the season when Joe decided to step down and retire.

His family was very concerned about Joe's health and wanted him to retire. I don't think he was burned out, but he made the right move and got out when he could. As I have said before, he was a big auto racing fan, and he got into that on a major scale when he got out of football and is still very involved in that today.

Our defensive coordinator, Richie Pettibone, took over, and he just had incredibly bad luck. He was one of the brightest coaching minds in the game, and when I was coaching the Cardinals, I always looked forward to the challenge of playing the Redskins because I knew Richie was going to have a great defensive game plan ready for us. It was like a chess match, seeing whether we could outthink him or not.

As the head coach, however, Richie took over a team that just got old together all of a sudden. We also had an incredible rash of injuries, especially to the offensive line. We were playing guys whose names we hardly knew. I looked over at the locker that had been Joe's the previous year and thought, "Joe baby, I didn't think you were smarter than me, but I guess you are."

All of the blame fell on Richie and it wasn't his fault. It was the fault of everybody in the organization, from the scouts and development people to the coaches and players. We didn't have new people ready to take over when those guys got old and lost a step or got hurt. The result was a 4-12 season, and Richie got fired.

Norv Turner was selected as the head coach, and I really thought he was going to be able to turn things around. The organization tried to bring in some young talent and went through some trying times, but it never did get back to where the franchise had been under Joe. We went 3-13 in 1994, and lost 11 of 12 games in the middle of the season. The next year, 1995, we were a little better, going 6-10.

The following season, 1996, we lost our opener to the Eagles, 17-14, but then proceeded to win seven games in a row. We were 7-1, and it was one of the most God-awful 7-1's you could ever see. We were really lucking out, there was no way we deserved to be 7-1. Our luck ran out, however, as we won only two of the final eight games and finished at 9-7.

One of the things I enjoyed most about coaching with the Redskins was the camaraderie of the coaches and players, and that was never more evident than after games, when many people on the team went to dinner at the same restaurant, The Alpine, in Arlington. The chef and owner, Ermano Tonizzo, is a great

Redskins fan. The other people would sing "Hail to the Redskins," and it was just a great atmosphere.

Our final game of the season was against Dallas, and we won easily, 37-10. I knew it was going to be the last game at RFK Stadium but I had no way of knowing it was going to be my final game with the Redskins. I was planning on finishing my career there.

RFK was a great stadium, and after the game the fans flooded the field and were trying to take any kind of souvenirs they could grab. They were actually grabbing patches of sod and stuffing it in their pockets.

We went to dinner at The Alpine, and this fellow came up to me and was talking about the game, and he was carrying this little paper bag. He said, "Coach I got down on the field after the game and I got some of the Redskin sod. Coach, I want you to have it."

I thanked him for the offer but told him he should keep it. He insisted, so I took it and I've still got it. I have nothing but happy memories of my years with the Redskins.

As I said, I really had never thought about leaving Washington, and if I had thought about it, there probably was only one place I would have left for—St. Louis. I really enjoyed the relationship with Norv Turner and the rest of the staff. I truly believed Norv would get the program turned around.

When Dick Vermeil came out of the broadcast booth and agreed to be the coach of the Rams, I was surprised but I also thought it was a good choice. I had known Dick for a long time— Coryell had wanted to hire him for his staff in St. Louis when we all joined the Cardinals in 1973—and respected his knowledge and passion for the game.

I wasn't prepared for him to call and ask me if I would be interested in joining his staff, but he did! I flew to St. Louis to meet with him, and Rick Smith, the Rams' public relations director, had a news conference scheduled even before I agreed to a contract. I was waiting to make sure the Redskins weren't going to make a counter offer, but Norv finally called back and said he had talked to Cooke and that he was sorry to see me go, but he understood.

About a week later, when I was back in Washington wrapping up my business there, Norv came by and asked me if I had talked to Cooke. Thinking back to my exit from San Diego and the confrontation with Klein, I picked up the phone and called him.

When he answered, I said, "Mr. Cooke, Jim Hanifan calling." He said, "You mean the traitor?" I said, "Oh jeez, Mr. Cooke," but before I could continue he interrupted me, "God-dammit, I paid you well here."

"I know that, Mr. Cooke," I said. "I had a wonderful time here and I appreciate it all, but I just had a chance to go back to my home town."

By that point he had calmed down. "I know that Jim," he said. "I understand and I don't blame you. That's what you should have done."

I was going back to St. Louis, which I really did consider home, when I didn't think it would ever be possible again. It was a dream come true.

CHAPTER 8

Back to St. Louis

When the opportunity developed to come to St. Louis and work with Dick Vermeil, it was a no-brainer. I never thought it would happen, but unbelievably, it did!

When I left St. Louis in 1987 for the job with the Falcons, I didn't think I would ever be back. I certainly didn't think I would be back after Bidwill pulled up and moved the Cardinals to Phoenix in 1987. I didn't think St. Louis would ever get another NFL team in my lifetime.

I had come back to St. Louis numerous times for different reasons over the years, for charity events or for NFL Alumni meetings, and each time I reminisced about my years with the Cardinals. One time I even went to Busch Stadium but I couldn't get in, so I just walked around the stadium. I've actually only been at Busch one time since I left, for a baseball game in 2003. I would like to go there when it's not baseball season and not crowded, so I could walk around and think about all of the happy times. I spent a long period of my life in that stadium. If they ever do tear it down and build a new stadium for the Cardinals it will be a sad day in my life.

When the Rams decided to move to St. Louis in 1995, I was thrilled for the city. I knew how many great football fans there were in St. Louis and how starved they were for a team. Along with that, so many ex-Cardinals players had become St. Louis residents, and they felt abandoned by the NFL!

We had two occasions to come back to St. Louis when I was with the Redskins, in 1995 and 1996, and it was amazing. I was on the field early, during the pre-game warmup, and fans were yelling to me from the stands, "Hey Jim," and waving. My linemen were in shock. "These people here really know you," they said. "You can't have that many friends here."

One of the games was when Dan Dierdorf was being inducted into the Rams' Ring of Honor at halftime. Even though he didn't play for the Rams, the organization was honoring a lot of former St. Louis Cardinals as a way to incorporate the football history in St. Louis with the Rams.

When we came back on the field for the start of the second half, all of these former players of mine were there and they were crowding around me and hugging me. We were still in the end zone, and I was afraid we were going to get a 15-yard penalty. It really did make me feel good to feel the love.

Dan had been kind enough to ask me to be his presenter at the Hall of Fame induction ceremonies in Canton, Ohio in 1996, and it was really special because Joe Gibbs was being inducted as well. Norv Turner let me miss a few days of training camp to go to Canton. A lot of head coaches would not have been so generous, and I really appreciated it.

It was even more special for Dan because Canton is his hometown. We were in the car, in the parade, when he saw a high school band and he said, "That's my band, my high school band." What an unbelievable thrill the whole weekend was for him. It was quite an experience just to be the presenter. Don Coryell was the presenter for Gibbs. With people like that, plus Conrad, Joe

Jacoby, Jim Lachey and Tommie Banks there, it really was like an old-home week.

The chance to come back to St. Louis was really special, and it was even more meaningful to have a chance to work with Dick. When I was the head coach of the Cardinals, Dick was coaching the Eagles. My first win as head coach was against Vermeil and the Eagles, at Busch. We shook hands after the game on the field, and I didn't expect to see him again until late in the season.

About an hour after the game, I was in the training room. Almost everybody was gone, and there was a knock on the side door. When I opened it, Dick was standing there. He came in and said, "Hey that was a heck of a job out there today, and I wanted to compliment you."

That was a special thing for him to do, and it really meant a lot to me. That is the kind of guy Dick Vermeil is. He is a great coach, but he is a better friend. Dick really views his coaching staff and players as family, the way it used to be in the old days. It doesn't happen that way very much any more in the NFL, but it still does with Dick.

When we had a retirement party for him after he retired as the Rams' coach following the 1999 season, he told me how much he remembered something I did for him when we were struggling in his early days with the Rams.

As he reiterated, he happened to walk by me in the hallway, after a team meeting. He said I told him, "You know what? You are one tough SOB."

Dick said, "For you to tell me that really made my day. It really picked me up when I needed it. You didn't know it, but it helped me immeasurably."

Those first two years with the Rams were very tough years. Dick put together an incredible staff—there were five guys working as assistants who had been head coaches in the NFL— myself, Al Saunders, Mike White, Frank Gansz and Bud Carson. Dick wanted those guys around him because they were good coaches, and he wasn't scared or intimidated by the fact they had been head coaches. He knew all of us on a social level, but more important was his respect for our football knowledge and coaching ability.

One of the first things Dick did was to call a meeting for everybody in the organization, from the front office down to the custodial staff, and there must have been 100 or more people in the room. Dick made a speech, and said that he wanted to make one point very clear to everybody —the most important people in the building were the players and coaches. "Make sure you understand that," he said. I'll bet that hit a lot of people right between the eyes. That was how Dick felt, and he didn't try to sugarcoat it.

One of the things that has changed about the game in 30 years is the number of support people working for an organization. We always had a public relations department, but nobody had heard of marketing the way clubs operate today. What I think some people forget is that what your marketing department is selling is your football team, and what sells is winning football. Some people think they are having such great success because they are unbelievable salesmen, but the team being successful is what is really responsible for the sales.

Those first two years with the Rams, 1997 and 1998, we had some players who just didn't work out, for whatever reason, like Lawrence Phillips and Tony Banks. Dick tried everything he could to help Phillips, and the young man did have some special skills. He got banged up, and his off-field problems finally got the best of him.

Dick was also very loyal to Banks, our quarterback, but our offense just continued to have major problems. If you don't have a guy under center who can get the job done, your offense is going to struggle. Tony Banks was a heck of an athlete, but for whatever reason he just couldn't get the job done. It seemed something bad was always happening to him, like a fumble or an interception. My linemen would come off the field and say, "What happened?" I would answer, "You'll see it tomorrow. I don't even want to get into it. You'll see it on the film."

We were 5-11 in 1997 and 4-12 in 1998, and I really thought the offensive assistants were going to get fired. The defense wasn't bad, so I thought those coaches were probably safe, but to send a message to the fans that the team was serious about winning, I thought the offensive coaches, including me, would be fired. The NFL does truly stand for Not For Long. In the end two coaches did leave, Jerry Rhome and Dick Coury. Both men are outstanding coaches, but it was their turn in the barrel.

One of the new assistants Dick hired was Mike Martz, who had been the quarterback coach in Washington, to come in as offensive coordinator. Mike and I had just missed each other with the Redskins, with him coming in as I was leaving. Norv had recommended him for the job as had Ernie Zampese, and those endorsements carried a lot of weight.

Just as so many things had gone wrong for us the previous two years, getting Martz was one of the first of a series of things that went right. Mike was able to talk the Rams management into signing free-agent quarterback Trent Green, a St. Louis kid who had been with the Redskins. John Shaw made a great trade with Indianapolis to bring in Marshall Faulk. We signed Adam Timmerman away from Green Bay to play right guard, and picked up another lineman, Andy McCollum, who had been cut by New Orleans. With our first pick in the draft, we selected a wide receiver to play opposite Isaac Bruce, Torry Holt. Suddenly, we had a terrific offense. Another assistant that Dick hired was John Matsko, who works with me with the offensive line. John's a terrific coach and a great friend. We're now going into our fifth year together. Prior to John, I had the pleasure of working with George Warhop and Ed White, my former player.

The attitude of the team was entirely different than it had been the year before. Through the first couple of preseason games,

Trent was playing terrific, Marshall was showing what kind of running back he was, and everybody was thinking maybe we had something special going.

Then came a game against the San Diego Chargers, and Rodney Harrison, their safety, came through on a blitz. He didn't mean to do it, but he dove recklessly and hit Trent's knee just as he was planting his leg to throw. Trent was lying on the astroturf and you knew immediately it was a bad injury. We knew before we left the stadium that night that Trent was gone for the year.

Usually after a home game I go to Dierdorf and Hart's restaurant, but I was just sick. I came home, sat down at the kitchen table and was very disconsolate. It was like somebody had put a curse on us. I sat there and could not get my mind straight, and couldn't take my mind away from the play and watching Trent writhing on the ground. I think he had only thrown three incomplete passes the entire preseason, and one of those came on a drop. The same thought kept coming into my head, "What are we going to do, what are we going to do?"

Two people did a marvelous job of talking to the team and the media and convincing everybody the season wasn't over—Dick Vermeil and Mike Martz. Both of them said they were very confident this other young quarterback we had signed, Kurt Warner, was going to be able to do the job. Dick talked to the entire team and Mike to the offense and sold them on the fact we were going to be fine. Dick said, "This is why everybody in this room has to be prepared, you backups never know when something like this is going to happen."

Some coaches on the staff were trying to lobby Dick about bringing in a veteran quarterback, but both Dick and Mike were confident in their opinion Kurt could do the job.

We went to Detroit for the final preseason game, and Kurt played OK, but not great. The team played OK, but since it was a preseason game, there was not a complete evaluation, because players kept moving in and out of the lineup. We were set to start the regular season, ready or not.

Our first game was against Baltimore, and I don't think we realized how good the Ravens were going to be in a couple of years, but they didn't know anything about us, either. Nobody knew what we had, and to a degree I don't think we knew it, either. What I remember most about the game, however, was when Kurt threw an interception down near the goal line. The Ravens took the ball and went down and scored.

I was on the sideline, talking to the linemen about the drive, when I heard someone trying to get my attention. "Coach, coach, can I talk to the guys a minute?" I turned around and it was Kurt. "Sure, go ahead," I said.

"Guys, that was my fault," Kurt said. "I'm sorry, but I guarantee you I'm going to make it up. Hang in there with me."

The guys all nodded and said for him not to worry about it.

Looking back on it, that was the start of the bonding between Kurt and the rest of the team, even though I didn't realize it at the time. The young man showed me something, acknowledging his mistake to his teammates but also saying, "Hey, I'm coming back."

I hadn't heard any quarterback talk like that for a long period of time, probably since Mark Rypien was with the Redskins. Dan Fouts would have said something like that, and so would Jim Hart.

Then, Kurt went out and did it and got us the game. We got on a roll and kept going. By the time we played San Francisco, the Rams' biggest rival, but a team we could never beat, we were 3-0. When we jumped out in front of the 49ers 21-0 in the first quarter, Kurt was on fire. He was so unbelievable and accurate in his reads, and his throws were so accurate that the receivers never had to break stride, just catch the ball and keep running. It was a thing of beauty.

When we were up 21-0, I had to tease Vermeil. I walked up to him on the sideline and said, "I think the kid can play."

We won big, moving us to 4-0, and that was about the time the national media began to catch on to what was happening. The players and coaches on the team were doing the same thing. Everybody was having fun, and it was such a high-octane team, that everybody was high-fiving all the time and going bonkers.

The Kurt Warner story began to get a lot of attention, and deservedly so. Here he had come out of nowhere, having played in Europe and the Arena League, and he only got his chance because of Trent Green's injury. To be honest, this was the type of season we thought Trent would have, not Kurt Warner. The fact that he had such an interesting personal story as well, having worked at a grocery store in between Arena League seasons, only made the press that much more interested in him.

He made a play in the 49er game that I still find hard to believe. He looked to his right and didn't like what he saw. He took his time, and the linemen were doing a great job in protecting him. He looked back the other way, and hit Isaac for about a 50-yard gain. He had so much confidence that the other players fed off it, and with Marshall doing his thing, it really was beautiful to watch.

Billy Long, who worked at Southern University but helped out with our weight program, came up with a slogan that the team quickly adopted—Gotta Go To Work. London Fletcher, one of our linebackers, was the catalyst of the defense and before every game in the locker room he got the chant going. "OK, fellas, got to go to work," he said.

By this time, we knew we had something special going. We were 6-0 before we lost a tough game at Tennessee, then followed that up by not playing well and losing at Detroit. Nobody panicked, however, and a win the following week at Carolina got us back on another roll. We won seven games in a row, raising our record to a league-best 13-2, and clinching the first-round bye and home-field advantage throughout the playoffs. We lost the final game of the year, at Philadelphia, but it truly was meaningless.

We beat Minnesota in the first round, then faced Tampa Bay in the NFC Championship Game. The Buccaneers had a great defense, and we expected a tough struggle. It was, too, and we didn't pull out the win until Kurt hit Ricky Proehl in the end zone in the final minutes for an 11-6 victory. It was Ricky's only touchdown of the year and it came at the perfect time.

It was a great play by both Ricky and Kurt, but the fans and the media missed one thing that happened on the play or it most likely would not have been successful. The Bucs had a blitz on, meaning they had four guys coming in, and we only had three to block them. Orlando Pace saw the safety coming, and bought enough time after blocking his defensive end to slide over and hit the safety just as he was about to get to Kurt. If Orlando doesn't make that play, Kurt would have been hit and the ball most likely would have fallen incomplete. Whether or not we would have won the game would have been a big question. The coaches knew it, and so did Kurt and the rest of the players.

We were going to the Super Bowl. In all of my years of coaching in St. Louis, it had finally happened. The city really is a great baseball town, and there are a lot of soccer fans as well, but the success of that Rams team made everybody a football fan.

Our opponent was Tennessee, a team that had beaten us earlier in the year. Dick, Mike White and the players left on Monday morning for Atlanta, the site of the game, but the rest of the coaches stayed behind to work on the game plan. We flew down on Tuesday night in two private planes, ready for the practices to begin on Wednesday. Unlike when I had been to the Super Bowl with the Redskins in 1991, we didn't have that extra week off to prepare for the game. It was coming up only one week later, and I think the lack of a layoff was one of the reasons why it was such a good game.

Critics have said it might have been the best Super Bowl game ever played. Kurt hit Isaac for a long touchdown, and just when it looked like the Titans were going to come back and tie the game, Mike Jones made a game-saving tackle on the final play of the game and we had won, 23-16.

It was a good game, but it shouldn't have been that close. We had some offensive opportunities that we had made all year but didn't make this time. We really were a couple of dropped balls away from making the game a blowout. If we had been farther ahead, the Titans would not have been able to just hand the ball off to Eddie George all the time.

It truly was an amazing conclusion to an unbelievable season. I am sure that someday there will be people who say, "I knew all along Kurt Warner would be the MVP and the Rams would win the Super Bowl." Yeah right, please. It was so special because nobody had any idea it was going to happen.

I was really proud of all of my linemen, because they did such a terrific job. Fred Miller, Adam Timmerman, Mike Gruttadauria, Tom Nutten and Orlando Pace were the regulars, along with Andy McCollum, and like most linemen, they were almost anonymous, but I know we would not have won without all of them playing extremely well.

We had a big party in Atlanta, then flew home Monday morning. The city had organized a parade, and I thought it would be nice, but I had no idea it would be as huge a celebration as it turned out to be. Schools closed early so the kids could come. When we got on the new Ram pickup trucks and the parade started down Market Street, I couldn't see anything but people. I don't know how many hundreds of thousands of fans were there.

Everybody was waving, but I actually could make out faces and hear people who I knew but hadn't seen since I came back to town. It brings tears to my eyes to think about it again. The whole town was celebrating, and there was no destruction or violence. That says a lot about the quality of people in St. Louis.

When the coaches came to work on Tuesday morning, we weren't surprised when Vermeil called a staff meeting. We thought he was going to give us some guidelines about the following weeks, when we could have some time off, etc. He walked in and said he wanted to thank all of us for our hard work and how it was such a great season. Then he delivered the reason for the meeting.

"Fellows, I think it's time for me to call it a day," Vermeil said. "I'm retiring. You will notice there is one coach who is not in this room. Mike Martz is downstairs signing a new contract as the new head coach of the Rams."

You talk about a shocker. I'm sure nobody on the staff had an inkling that was coming. I don't even know when he and Carol had talked about it, maybe the night before the game, saying if we win it, I'm going to retire. It was just so unexpected, because that is the time a coach usually does not retire, when he is on top of the heap.

Dick thought he was going to move back to his farm in Pennsylvania, near his children and grandchildren, so he and Carol could spend more time with them. He told me later that when they got back there, it didn't turn out the way they thought it would. They found out their kids had their own lives, and when Dick and Carol wanted to get together with them, the kids and grandkids had stuff going on. He said all of a sudden they were looking at each other thinking retirement wasn't what they thought it would be.

A year later, Dick shocked everybody again by coming back as the coach of the Kansas City Chiefs. I really do think he is happiest when he is coaching, because he really looks at his coaches and players as part of his family. That is kind of rare in this day and age, but that truly is the way Dick feels.

We weren't surprised that Mike was taking over. That agreement had already been reached between Mike and John Shaw that he would be the new coach when Dick retired; it was just that nobody was prepared for it to happen so soon.

Mike had received a lot of credit, and it was well deserved, for our offensive success. Because of that we all knew the transition should be very smooth, because we were going to continue to do the same things that had worked so successfully in 1999.

Unfortunately, for a variety of reasons, we didn't play as well in 2000. We went 10-6 and made the playoffs on the final day of the season when we beat New Orleans while Chicago was upsetting Detroit. We had to go right back to New Orleans the next week, however, to play the Saints in the first round of the playoffs. We had won 35-21 in the final game of the year, and I'm sure the New Orleans coaches used that game as a great motivation during practice all week.

We didn't play well but still had a chance to come back and maybe win the game in the final minute when our punt returner, fumbled a punt and the Saints recovered. Had we scored and won the game, we really might have gotten on another roll and gone on to another Super Bowl, but it didn't happen. Sometimes one play like that really can make the difference in a season, especially if it happens in the playoffs. That is why coaches really stress the importance of every play, because you never know when a big or deciding moment is going to come.

Losing like that was a wakeup call, and I think it made everyone on the team more determined to get back to a Super Bowl level in 2001. It just reinforced how truly hard it is to get to the Super Bowl, and gave new status to those teams like the Steelers and 49ers that were able to win for so many years in a row. A lot of times players lose that motivational edge once they have won one Super Bowl, and for those players to keep that motivation and keep working as hard as you have to to be successful is a real credit to them and their coaches.

We still had a good group of guys, and we had fun during the season. The linemen got me one day. We always had boxes of Krispy Kreme donuts in our offensive line meeting, and I really try hard to resist them. The problem is if you eat one, you know you are going to eat about six before you stop. We were walking out of a meeting one day and there was only one donut left. I decided it wouldn't hurt, so I took a couple of bites out of it. I sat it back down because it didn't taste right. I wasn't sure what it was, it was just weird. I started to walk away, and then for some reason I went back and ate the rest of the donut.

Just as I put the last bite in my mouth, Ryan Tucker walked back in the room and stared at me. "You didn't eat that did you?" he asked. Then he burst out laughing. "You ate the donut with the wax on it." No wonder it didn't taste very good. They had set me up!

The disappointing way we were bounced out of the playoffs in 2000 gave us the motivation we needed for the 2001 season. We opened the year with an overtime win at Philadelphia, then went out and won at San Francisco.

We were going to play Miami in our home opener, and it was our first game at home since the September 11 tragedies. We were in a staff meeting the Thursday night before the game, and Mike said that the organization wanted to have somebody run onto the field before the game carrying the American flag. When we had played in San Francisco, they had a big ceremony where all of the players and coaches held this giant flag that almost covered the entire field. It was a very moving moment.

We were talking about who should do it, when somebody said, "Wait a minute, we're not thinking right. There is only one person who should carry the flag. There's only one of us who is a veteran, who spent time in the service, and that's Jim."

Mike looked at me and said, "Would you do that?" I didn't have to think about it. "I would be absolutely honored to do that," I said.

I have received a lot of honors in my life, but carrying the flag onto the field at the TWA Dome that day was one of the greatest thrills and greatest moments I've ever had in my life. I still get choked up every time I think about it.

The problem was, we never practiced what I was going to do, and I had no idea how heavy the flag pole was going to be. We were in the tunnel, ready to run onto the field, and I told the guys to make sure they gave me a little room before they came onto the field after me. I didn't want them screaming by me and knocking me down. I also was worried that I might stub my toe and trip and fall. That crossed my mind for a minute, and I said a short, silent prayer, "Please God, don't let that happen. It would be so embarrassing."

The moment came, and I took off and headed for midfield. I couldn't hear any of the announcements, but I could feel the crowd and hear the roar of the crowd. I've never really talked about it, but my heart really swelled. I was so proud to be an American.

I ran out there like my Irish/Viking ancestors, carrying the pole above my head, and that baby was heavy. I got to midfield and turned and presented it to all corners of the stadium, and I was thinking, "Somebody get off their duff and get out here and take this from me." I didn't want to have to reach up and grab it with my other arm. Finally somebody did.

We went out and won the game 42-10, and I was thinking more about the game when he met the Miami coaches at midfield after the game. The Miami offensive line coach, Tony Wise, said to me, "That was one of the greatest things I've ever seen, when you ran out there with that flag." That meant something to me, because we had just beaten them badly, but carrying that flag and our national response to the terrorist attacks was far more important than the result of a football game.

They had not shown me carrying the flag live during the television broadcast, but went to a tape of it later during the game. Dan Dierdorf was broadcasting the game. Afterward, I went to Dierdorf and Hart's restaurant, and everybody there was talking about it. I got calls from friends all over the country, including a lot of my buddies from the Army.

The terrorist attacks really brought America together. I went to my dentist's office, and while he was working on my tooth I told him, "You should go over to the Middle East and find those people and do to them what you are doing to me right now."

I didn't know anybody who died in the attacks, but months later I was able to meet some of the New York policemen and firemen when they came to St. Louis to be the honorary chairmen of our St. Patrick's Day parade. The stories they told were just incredible and amazing.

We stayed hot, winning our first six games before losing a tough game to one of our fiercest rivals, New Orleans. We had another six-game winning streak to end the regular season and finished the year 14-2, once again securing the first-round bye and homefield advantage throughout the playoffs.

Everybody was having fun again, and that was never more evident than the week after my University of California Bears played Mike Martz' Fresno State Bulldogs. Anytime coaches' schools play, we always have a little wager on the game. My wager with Mike was that whichever team won, the losing coach would have to wear the other school's clothes during practice one day.

Why Cal would even schedule Fresno State, I don't know, but they lost the game. Pat Hill is the head coach there, and I have known Pat since he was coaching high school football in southern California. He sent Mike a Fresno State sweatshirt and hat for me to wear in practice and I did. Unbeknownst to me, Mike had the public relations staff take a lot of photos of me in the Fresno State gear, and sent one of those pictures back to Pat to sit on his desk. It's still there!

I was thinking about what I could do for revenge. The next morning, I took the sweatshirt and hat and went into our maintenance shed and put them in a tray and gave them a dousing of paint thinner. I poured almost a gallon on that shirt and hat.

I carried it onto the field for the start of practice, trying to hide from Mike. The players saw me and were curious about what I was doing. As they all gathered around me, I pulled out a book of matches. "This is what you do to your competitors, your enemies," I said. I put the tray down, threw the book of matches on it and the whole thing burst into flames. The flames had to be five or six feet high. The team went crazy with laughter.

I really thought that was the end of it, that I had gotten even, or maybe even was up one. Two or three weeks went by, and people forgot about it.

We were in our Saturday meeting with the entire offense, and Mike was running the projector, looking at the film of Friday's practice. The room was dark, but all of a sudden Dan Linza, who is the Rams' director of security, came in, followed by two Missouri Highway Patrol officers. "Coach Martz, Coach Martz, we need to speak with you, please."

Mike stopped the projector and turned on the lights. He of course had set this up, so he wasn't surprised, he knew exactly what was going on. "Yes Chief, what is it?" Mike said.

The highway patrolmen had a very stern look and the room got very quiet. Linza said, "Coach, these fellows here have an arrest warrant for somebody in this room." Now, believe me, everybody was trying to hide. Then Linza said, "Would Jim Hanifan please come up here."

"What? Give me a break," I said.

"Jim, please come up here," Linza said. I started to walk to the front of the room, and our resident prankster, Adam Timmerman, yelled out, "I told you she wasn't 18." I gave Adam a dirty look and said, "Knock it off."

Everybody in the room was laughing, because they knew it wasn't them who had the problem. I got up to the officers and said, "OK, what's the deal, what's the charge?"

One of the officers was trying to put handcuffs on me and I said, "Hold it, we're not doing that." The other said the charge was destruction of property, "Fresno State property."

I then knew I had been had. "OK, that was pretty good," I said. And it was!

Everybody was confident and relaxed as the playoffs opened, and we rolled over Green Bay, then won a tough game against the Eagles for the NFC Championship. For the second time in three years, we were going to the Super Bowl, this time to play New England.

We were coming onto the field after the warmup, when I saw former President Bush and Roger Staubach standing near us. They were there for the pregame coin toss. I went over to them and gave Roger a big hug and shook hands with the President.

When we got onto the field, they were both standing on the sideline and for some reason there was a delay in the coin toss, so I went over to talk to them. My friend Ray Ogas was standing a few feet away from me, and he heard my conversation.

I was just chatting with President Bush and Ray heard me say, "Well, you know you cheated on that, you and your ringer." I was talking about the night the Redskins went to the White House and he had won the horseshoes contest, but Ray didn't know that. The President and I were laughing back and forth.

Ray asked me about it later and he said, "I've known you forever, and you were talking with him like he was an old friend." I said I really think of the President that way, he and his wife are just such neat people.

Unfortunately that was the only highlight of the game. We lost 20-17 on a 48-yard field goal on the final play of the game. We had beaten the Patriots earlier in the year, and on the films we counted they blitzed 38 times. They tried everything to discombobulate us and nothing worked. Kurt threw for more than 400 yards, and I don't know if they ever touched him.

New England changed its strategy for the game and never blitzed once. They jammed the heck out of our receivers, holding them and grabbing them. They mauled our receivers and got away with it. That was their game plan, just to rape them, and it was well into the second half before they were called for holding. Even after all of that, we scored late to tie the game, and all we had to do on their last drive was tackle somebody and not let them continue to run out of bounds. If we could have got the game into overtime, maybe we could have won.

That was one of the most disappointing games I was ever involved in, ranking with the loss to Washington in 1985 that cost the Cardinals the division title, the San Diego loss to Houston in the playoffs in 1979 and the Rams' loss to New Orleans in the 2000 playoffs.

It is always hard to predict what a team is going to do before the season begins. One reporter asked me one time what I thought would happen and I said, "I think we're going to go 16-0 in the regular season, then win three games in the playoffs and win the Super Bowl, 19-0 that's it." The man just stood there with an open mouth. Of course I didn't believe it, but you get tired of people asking you. The truth is you never know how you are going to do, because there are so many things that can happen. You can sit down before the year begins and say, "These are the given problems, but where are the hidden ones?"

The hidden problems in 2002 were all of the injuries we suffered, starting right with the opening game against Denver. Adam Timmerman had a sore knee, but I didn't catch it and neither did John Matsko, our other line coach, until the pre-game warmup, and by then it was too late. There were two times Kurt had a chance to make a big play, but he didn't get the time he needed to complete the pass. We lost the game, and Mike Martz got criticized for going for a first down on fourth down when we could have kicked a field goal to tie the game. It was a play that almost always works, but this time it didn't—because the Denver cornerback fell down and found himself in a different spot on the field, covering a different receiver than he should have been covering.

As much as the little things sometimes get a team on a winning streak, it can happen just as easily in reverse, and that's what happened to us in 2002. We lost our first five games of the year, and Kurt Warner went out with a broken finger. We also lost Orlando Pace for six weeks because of an injury. We had not experienced anything like that for several years, and suddenly there was griping and bitching and complaining going on everyday. The media was being critical, and it was something none of us were enjoying.

Suddenly, we had a breath of fresh air when Marc Bulger came out of nowhere to replace Warner at quarterback. He won five consecutive games, and suddenly we were back to 5-5 and everybody was saying great things about us again. It was like Warner all over again, it was truly amazing. I thought, "We must really be drinking some good water around here."

Unfortunately the good times didn't last, and we lost four of our last six games to finish the year at 6-10, missing the playoffs for the first time in four years.

I think it proved to everybody how humbling the NFL can be, and that you can never be certain what is going to happen from one year to the next, even with the same players. A team's chemistry can be entirely different, and things can go poorly just as easily as they can go well.

The poor performance was not totally discouraging, however, because we believed in ourselves, and our talent, and will enter the 2003 season fully expecting to bounce back and be a contending team once again.

The players on the Rams, and the coaches, have a tremendous amount of pride, and I, for one, expect great things to happen this year.

Dick Vermeil and Mike Martz talk about their friend, Jim Hanifan.

When I came back into coaching with the Rams, Jim was the first guy I thought of trying to get on our staff. Jim brings so much more than Xs and Os to a team and to an offensive line. His credentials go way beyond being able to coach the offensive line, and he contributes far more to the overall team. He makes a wonderful contribution to the team's chemistry.

He is a very loyal friend. You can not see him for four years, and if you call up and say you need him he will be there. He can chew out a guy and have him smiling at the same time. You always know that Jim is going to do what is best for the team. He really cares about all of his players.

He is one of the best at teaching the Xs and Os, but a lot of coaches can do that. Very few add the dimension of chemistry that he adds.

Dick Vermeil received a lot of credit for the Rams' success, but he wouldn't have achieved that without Jim Hanifan. I love the guy. I will always be indebted to him.

— Dick Vermeil

Jim Hanifan is a lot of fun. We had not worked together until I came to the Rams, although I certainly knew of him. When I was in college he would come out to Fresno State to work out prospects before the draft, and I knew he was one of the most highly revered coaches in the league.

I can't imagine him at 25 being any different than he is now. When he gets on the practice field it looks like he has had three pints of coffee. He just doesn't stop. The offensive line has more people than any other position, which is why we have two coaches there. He and John Matsko work so well together. They are like

the two professors sitting up in the box on the *Muppet Show.*
They look at tape together and compliment each other back and
forth—it makes you want to gag.

We were worried about Jim one night, in 1999. I came upstairs
to the offices and Jim was leaning against the railing and said he
felt a little dizzy. He was out of breath and it didn't sound—good
to me, so we called 911. The paramedics wanted to take him to
the emergency room, and he didn't want to go. He was John
Wayne all the way. He faked like he was falling down when they
tried to get him on the gurney, but they didn't think it was funny.

He was still smoking and wearing all of this cheap cologne
and stuffing 15 pieces of gum in his mouth to try to cover it up.
We got the name of his cardiologist and his phone number and
wrote it in eight-inch red letters and numbers on the board next
to our game plan. We told him we wanted to know who to call
quickly if something happened to him. He had to look at that
every day. Finally he did quit.

Jim should have been in politics. He is extremely intelligent,
and with his personality, you can't help but like him. I don't know
anybody who doesn't like him. It's amazing to watch the other
line coaches gather around him when we are at the scouting
combine or places like that. He just sits there and holds court.

We have a Hanifan rule. You can never let him get between
you and the door. One time he started telling me a story, followed
me into the shower, kept telling the story while I got dressed and
followed me up to my office. He was still telling the same story.

We call him the mayor of St. Louis. We will be walking
together, and people will walk right past me to ask him for his
autograph. He is such a great teacher and has such a terrific
relationship with his players.

He does plan to step away a little bit after this season, and he
needs to. There's so much life in him. He's got so many things he
wants to do. He and Mariana need to take that time to go have

fun together, but he will definitely be missed. There is only one Hani.

—*Mike Martz*

CHAPTER 9

Looking Ahead

I am going into the 2003 season expecting it to be my final year of coaching.

It's exciting, because I don't know what is going to happen. I will sit down with John Shaw and Mike Martz after the season and talk about it and figure out what I want to do.

A lot of fans don't realize how hard coaches—at all levels—work. They think we waltz out there and play the game. If you don't have a passion for the game, it is going to be hard to put in the hours necessary to be successful. I still have that passion, but I think I might be pushing the envelope a little bit. Fans don't see us working at 2:00 a.m.

I look back at my high school coaches, and they retired when they were 55. A lot of coaches get out of coaching when they are in their 50s and go into scouting. Coryell's staff, in St. Louis and San Diego, are all retired except for me. All of my staff when I was a head coach are retired. There are only a couple of us left coaching who were on Joe Gibbs's staff in Washington.

Whatever happens, I know I am not the type of person who will sit around and mess with the garden or play bridge or chess. I love golf, but I can't play it everyday. Then it becomes a job. I don't know what I'm going to do, but I have a lot of thoughts about what I might do.

I have thought about doing some work in radio or television, but I don't know if I would be good at it. I've thought about having some camps for either linemen coming out of college or for free agents who are hoping to find a job. I am going to investigate those things and see what develops.

I want to travel. I definitely want to go to Ireland and see my cousins. I want to spend more time with my kids and my grandson, Austin, who is in junior high and just completed his first football camp at Colorado State. I know I am going to have those opportunities and I am excited about it.

Both of my children, Kathy and Jim, live in Colorado. Kathy and her husband Bill own the Elk River Guest Ranch in Steamboat Springs and they are going into their ninth year there. They have had to work hard to make it a success, but they are doing something they enjoy doing. She really did what she said she was going to do years ago—find a job just like her dad, a job that doesn't seem like work.

Jimmy has three different businesses going. He and his partner own a special events center outside Denver that is already booked for every weekend through 2004, mostly for weddings. They spent five years getting everything ready, and it is just a beautiful place. He also makes terrific artwork out of steel, and he is a ski and snowboard instructor in the winter.

Whatever I do, I will be watching a lot of football games. You would think there would not be any more refinements that could be made to the game, but I know there will be some. The players keep getting bigger and faster, and it's amazing today that we see quarterbacks like Dante Culpepper. He is a huge man, and he can run like a deer and throw. That's been the evolution of the game, seeing players become that athletic, and I know that is going to continue.

One thing hasn't changed—football is a great game, and a fun game. It's a game that develops a lot of character. A player can learn a lot of lessons from the game. People walk away from the game with more than they had when they started, and I'm not talking about the financial aspect of it.

I'm so glad I did what I did and went into coaching. It was the right thing for me, no question. I truly loved playing it, and I have loved coaching it. I enjoyed my teammates and I enjoyed the players on all of my teams.

I will miss the camaraderie that comes from being part of a team. I will miss the pranks. I will miss teaching, and watching a young player learning how to play and getting better and better.

Football is much more than the Xs and Os; it's the people involved who have made my life so enjoyable. I can only think of one thing to say to everybody who has been part of this great ride—thank you.

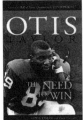

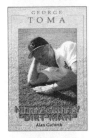

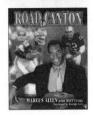